Cooking with Interest

First printed in 2005 10 9 8 7 6 5 4 3 2 1
Printed in Canada

The Publisher: Kicking Horse Press Ltd.

National Library of Canada Cataloguing in Publication

Cooking with interest /

Collection of recipes from employees of the Royal Bank of Canada as a fundraiser for the United Way.

Includes index.

ISBN-13: 978-0-9739562-0-7
ISBN-10: 0-9739562-0-8

1. Cookery. II. Title.

TX715.6.C66925 2005 641.5 C2005-907025-0

Project Director: Nicholle Carrière
Proofreader: Sherrin Berezowsky
Production: HR Media Ltd., Willa Kung

PC: Nisku Printers Ltd.

CONTENTS

DEDICATION

This cookbook is dedicated to United Way of the Alberta Capital Region and the many wonderful agencies and causes it supports within each community.
RBC Royal Bank is very proud to be associated with the United Way Group.

We would like to thank all the employees in Edmonton and the surrounding area for supplying us with their favourite recipes. Your support is greatly appreciated and has made our cookbook a wonderful collection of interesting recipes. Many of the staff have listed their names in the book and some of them have chosen not to have their names published.

We hope everyone enjoys preparing these terrific recipes as much as we enjoyed preparing the cookbook.

Thank you for your continued support!

RBC Royal Bank United Way Special Events Committee
Carrie, Deb, Jamie, Maria, Daniel, Janet, Brad and Dan

A RECIPE FOR FRIENDSHIP

1 C of Friendly Words
1 C of Courtesy and Patience
2 Heaping C of Understanding

Sift carefully to remove all the malice and ego, add a dash of wit and humour.

A pinch of warm personality, a handful of forgiveness and an ounce of praise.

Mix well until blended.

Cook slowly, keep temperatures low, no boiling, steaming or stewing is necessary.

Season to taste with the spice of life.

Top each serving with a goodly amount of kindness, a little bit of love and tolerance improves the flavour. Serve in generous portions!

PLAY DOUGH

1 C flour
1/2 C salt
2 Tsp cream of tartar
1 C water
1 T oil
Food colouring

Cook in pot until mixture forms a ball (stirring at all times). Remove dough and knead it. Store in a plastic bag in the fridge. Great fun for kids to play with.

Appetizers & Side Dishes

Sharon Mohr
Fort Saskatchewan Branch—05839

SHRIMP BUNS

1 can shrimp, drained
1 can cream of mushroom soup
1 T chopped green onion
Dash of garlic salt or roast garlic
4 crusty buns, cut in half and buttered
Grated Cheddar cheese

Preheat broiler. Mix all ingredients and distribute on 8 bun halves. Top with grated Cheddar cheese and broil until cheese is melted.

Laverne Snoek
Heritage Branch—04089

SPINACH DIP

2 C sour cream
1 C Miracle Whip
3 green onions, chopped
1 pkg frozen chopped spinach
1 pkg Knorr vegetable soup mix
1 small tin water chestnuts, chopped
Round loaf of sourdough bread
Sourdough buns

Mix all ingredients together except breads. Cut top off round loaf of bread. Remove inside and chop into bite-sized pieces. Pour dip into bread bowl. Chop buns into bite-sized pieces. Dip may be stored in refrigerator up to 1 week. If you don't have bread, use crackers.

Cheryl Leverette
Mayfield Business Banking Centre—03839

HOT BEAN DIP

1–14 oz can refried beans
1–250 g pkg cream cheese
1 C sour cream
1 T chopped chives
1 T chopped onion
1 T parsley
2 T chili powder
1 1/2 C grated Monterey Jack and Cheddar cheese
1 to 2 T chili powder

Preheat oven to 350 degrees F. Combine beans, cream cheese, sour cream, onion, chives, parsley and chili powder. Spread in low baking dish. Sprinkle with cheese and additional 2 T chili powder. Bake for approximately 25 minutes, until bubbly. Serve with tortilla chips or crackers.

Barbara Chandler
Sherwood Park Branch—05489

HAM BALL

1–8 oz pkg cream cheese
1/4 C mayonnaise
2–8 oz cans flaked ham
2 T chopped parsley
1 Tsp minced onion
1/4 Tsp dry mustard
1/4 Tsp Tabasco sauce

Mix the above ingredients thoroughly. Divide in half and make 2 balls. Roll in finely chopped walnuts. Chill. Serve with crackers. I often put one ball in the freezer for later.

Myrna Buck
Sherwood Park Branch—05489

WONTON FLOWERS

24 wonton wrappers
1 pkg (4 to 5) big Italian sausages
1 C medium salsa
1/2 C shredded Monterey Jack cheese
1/2 C shredded medium cheese
Sour cream (for topping)
Green onion (chopped, for topping)

Preheat oven to 350 degrees F. Take sausage meat out of casing and cook. Add the salsa and both cheeses to cooked sausage meat. Mix well.

Line mini muffin tins with wrappers. Add 1 T of mixture into each wonton. Cook 8 to 10 minutes. Sprinkle chopped green onion and a teaspoon of sour cream on top.

Rossana Vojacek
Sherwood Park Branch—05489

ERIN'S APPLE DIP

2/3 C brown sugar
500 g Philadelphia cream cheese
1/2 C SKOR bits
1–250 g container of caramel
3 to 4 Granny Smith apples

Beat the cream cheese and brown sugar together, and spread on a platter. Heat up the caramel for 30 seconds in the microwave, and spoon over cream cheese. Sprinkle SKOR bits on top and presto! Cut apples in thin wedges and dip in!

Audrey Fredrickson
Devon Branch—03419

ULTIMATE BRUSCHETTA

8 to 10 ripe plum tomatoes
2 T finely chopped onion
2 large garlic cloves, minced
1/4 C chopped fresh basil
2 Tsp red wine vinegar
6 T extra virgin olive oil
Salt and pepper
4 thick slices crusty Italian bread

Cut tomatoes in half, and squeeze out seeds and juice. Chop tomatoes into small dice; place in bowl. Add onion, garlic, basil, vinegar, half of the olive oil and salt and pepper to taste. Let stand at room temperature for about 1 hour. Drain liquid. On barbecue grill or under broiler, toast bread on both sides until golden brown. Quickly brush one side of each slice with remaining olive oil. Spoon tomato mixture on top. Cut slices in half. Serve immediately.

A Bachelor
Edmonton Main Branch—03749

COCA-COLA CHICKEN WINGS

2 dozen chicken wings
2 cans Coke
Salt and pepper

Season chicken wings with salt and pepper. Pan-fry both sides on high heat until golden brown (the inside can still be raw). Cover wings with Coke. Put the lid on the pan and cook, stirring often. Serve when you think the wings are cooked. Serve hot.

Deb Owens
Edmonton Main Branch—03749

MARINATED FETA AND SUN-DRIED TOMATO BITES

1/4 C drained and very finely diced oil-packed sun-dried tomatoes
1/4 C finely chopped fresh basil
2 T finely chopped pitted Kalamata olives
2 Tsp balsamic vinegar
1/2 Tsp coarsely ground black pepper
1/4 to 1/2 Tsp crushed red chili flakes (optional)
2 large garlic cloves, minced
1/3 C extra virgin olive oil
1 1/3 C coarsely crumbled feta cheese
2 small English cucumbers

In a bowl, stir tomatoes with basil, olives, vinegar, pepper, chili flakes (if using), garlic and oil. Add cheese and stir evenly to coat. Cover tightly and refrigerate for at least 6 hours or up to 2 days for flavours to meld.

Drag lines of a fork down sides of each cucumber to make ridges. Then cut cucumbers into 1/2 -inch slices. Using a melon baller or a small spoon, create a bowl in the centre of each slice. Pat each slice dry and store in the refrigerator until needed, for up to 1 day. Then spoon enough cheese mixture into each cucumber cup to make a nicely rounded serving. Arrange on a platter.

It's best to serve right away, but if making ahead, loosely cover with plastic wrap and refrigerate. Cucumber softens as it sits, but will be fine for up to 4 hours.

Jessica
Southgate Shopping Centre Branch—04359

THAI PIZZA ON A GARLIC CRUST

Crust:
325 ml all-purpose flour
5 ml instant yeast
2 ml salt
1 ml garlic powder
125 ml hot water
15 ml cooking oil

Topping:
60 ml peanut sauce
175 ml grated part-skim mozzarella cheese
140 to 170 g boneless, skinless chicken breast
1 medium carrot, julienned
0.5 ml cayenne pepper
15 ml cooking (or chili-flavoured) oil
1 large red pepper, cut into 8 rings
250 ml fresh bean sprouts, washed and blotted dry
3 green onions, sliced diagonally
5 ml sesame seeds, toasted

Food Processor Method for Crust: Measure first four ingredients into food processor fitted with dough blade. With motor running, pour hot water and first amount of cooking oil through food chute. Process for 50 to 60 seconds. If dough seems sticky, turn out onto lightly floured surface. Knead, adding more flour as needed, until smooth and elastic. Cover with tea towel. Let dough rest for 15 minutes.

Hand Method: Combine first four ingredients in medium bowl. Add hot water and first amount of cooking oil. Mix well until dough pulls away from sides of bowl. Turn out onto lightly floured surface. Knead for 5 to 8 minutes, until smooth and elastic. Cover with tea towel. Let dough rest for 15 minutes.

To Complete: Preheat oven to 425 degrees F. Roll out crust and press into greased 12-inch (30 cm) pizza pan, forming rim around edge. Spread with peanut sauce. Sprinkle with cheese. Sauté chicken, carrot and cayenne pepper in second amount of cooking oil in frying pan for about 5 minutes, until chicken is no longer pink. Arrange over cheese.

Place red pepper around outside edge. Bake on bottom rack in oven for 15 minutes, until cheese is melted and crust is golden. Remove from oven. Sprinkle with bean sprouts, green onion and sesame seeds. Cut into 8 wedges.

Allison Laursen
Southgate Shopping Centre Branch—04359

HOT MUSHROOM DIP

3 C chopped mushrooms
1 C chopped onion
1 T dill
Dash of garlic
1–250 g pkg cream cheese
1 1/2 C shredded Monterey Jack cheese
1/2 C mayonnaise
2 to 3 green onions, chopped

Preheat oven to 350 degrees F. Fry mushrooms, onion, dill and garlic for 10 minutes. Add cheeses and mayo; stir and bake in a casserole for about half an hour. Sprinkle green onions on top and serve with crackers.

Lahni Smith
Southgate Shopping Centre Branch—04359

SPINACH DIP

1 C sour cream
1 C mayonnaise
4 green onions, chopped
1 can water chestnuts, chopped
1 pkg frozen chopped spinach
1 pkg Knorr dried vegetable soup mix
1 round pumpernickel bread

Mix sour cream, mayo, green onions, water chestnuts and Knorr soup mix in a bowl and chill overnight. Thaw the spinach overnight and add to the mixture the next morning.

Preheat oven to 350 degrees F. Cut a hole in the round pumpernickel and scoop out the bread (you can cut this bread up and use it with the dip). Put the dip inside the bread bowl and wrap loaf in foil. Cook in the oven for 1 to 1 1/2 hours. Serve hot with crackers or the bread chunks from inside the loaf.

Jo Halaby
Area Office—04759

HOUMAS

1 can chick peas
2 heaping T sesame paste
Juice of 1 lemon
1/4 C olive oil
Garlic
Salt to taste

Mix all ingredients in a blender or food processor until the consistency of a thick paste. Chill and serve with toasted pita chips.

Chris Buckley
Operations and Market Place Support—03059

MEXICAN LAYER DIP

1 can refried beans
1/2 pkg taco mix
1/2 C sour cream
1/2 C mayonnaise
4 fresh tomatoes, diced
1 bunch green onions
Grated Cheddar cheese, enough to cover layer
Add diced peppers if you wish

Layer ingredients as follows. First layer: beans. Second layer: blend taco mix, sour cream and mayonnaise. Spread over beans. Third layer: diced tomatoes. Fourth layer: green onions (and peppers, if adding). Top layer: grated Cheddar cheese. Refrigerate until serving.

Sylvia Hooft
Meadowlark Centre Branch—04329

JAPANESE CHICKEN WINGS

3 lbs chicken wings
1 C flour
1 egg, beaten

Sauce:
3 T soy sauce
1 C white sugar
3 T water
1 Tsp Accent
1/2 Tsp salt
1/2 C vinegar

Preheat oven to 350 degrees F. Dip wings in egg. Coat in flour. Fry until brown. Lay in shallow pan. Combine all sauce ingredients and heat until dissolved. Pour sauce over wings and bake for 1 to 1 1/2 hours. Turn wings occasionally.

Pam Meaver
Lake District Branch—03869

CHICKEN LETTUCE WRAPS

Sauce:
3/4 C hoisin sauce
1 1/2 Tsp rice vinegar
1 T liquid honey
2 T water
1 T fresh lime juice
2 Tsp sesame oil
1 large garlic clove, minced
1 Tsp freshly grated ginger

Wraps:
2 boneless chicken breasts
1/3 C grated carrot
2 green onions, diagonally sliced
1 C dry steam-fried noodles (fine, crunchy cooked noodles)
1/2 C unsalted peanuts, chopped
1 head iceberg lettuce, separated into whole leaves, core removed

In a small saucepan, over medium-low heat, blend sauce ingredients. Set aside to cool. Poach chicken in a small amount of water until no longer pink. Cool. Cut each breast in half horizontally and then dice to about 1/4 inch. In medium bowl, toss chicken, carrots and onion with enough sauce to coat. Let stand for 15 minutes. Add noodles and peanuts; gently toss with more sauce to coat.

To Serve: Set out lettuce and chicken mixture. Let guests wrap their own. Serve extra sauce on the side.

Jennifer Langley
Edmonton Main Branch—03749

JEN'S BAKED ONION DIP

2 medium onions, finely chopped
1 C shredded Cheddar (or you can use pre-shredded cheese mix with mozzarella or Swiss as well)
1/2 C mayonnaise
Bacon (as much as you like—the more the better. I use the pre-cooked Maple Leaf bacon so you can just microwave it for a minute and chop the slices up into small pieces)
1/4 C grated Parmesan cheese
Wheat Thins crackers

Preheat oven to 350 degrees F. Mix onion, cheese, mayo and bacon bits until well blended. Spoon into a lightly greased shallow baking dish or a 9-inch pie plate. Sprinkle with the Parmesan cheese. Bake for 30 minutes or until lightly browned and bubbly. Serve with the crackers.

Note: You can make this ahead of time. Just cover and refrigerate up to 24 hours, and then uncover and bake as directed.

Alison Soby
Manulife Branch—04739

FIESTA PLATTER

1 to 2 ripe avocados
2 to 2 1/2 C salsa (1 full jar)
1/2 block light cream cheese
1 to 2 C sour cream
2 C or more Cheddar cheese, shredded
2 green onions, chopped
1 T lemon juice
1 T seasoning salt
1/2 to 1 Tsp garlic salt

1 bag of your favourite tortilla chips

Cut up avocado in a shallow pie dish and combine it with lemon juice, seasoning salt and garlic salt. Mash with a fork until smooth or however you like your guacamole.

Next, in a separate bowl, combine sour cream, chopped green onion and cream cheese. Mash with a fork until smooth, and layer this with spatula or spoon on top of the guacamole layer.

The third layer is the salsa; spoon it on evenly over the sour cream. Top with shredded Cheddar cheese, and chill in fridge to set until needed.

Serve with tortilla chips and you will be instantly transported to Mexico! Serves approximately 4 to 6 as an appetizer. Enjoy!

Extras: For a heartier appetizer or meal, add a can of refried beans to the bottom layer, or add 1 to 2 C cooked hamburger after the sour cream layer.

Tara Sohanpal
Edmonton Main Branch—03749

FISH TIKKAS

1 kg fish fillets, cut into cubes
Salt to taste
1 T lemon juice
1/2 C yogurt
1 T vinegar
1 T garam masala (from Superstore or East Indian store)
2 Tsp ground cumin seeds
1/2 Tsp carom
1 Tsp red chili powder
2 Tsp garlic paste
Oil or butter for basting

Wash and dry the cubed fish fillets. Sprinkle with salt and lemon juice. Set aside to marinate for half an hour.

In a bowl, combine yogurt with the remaining ingredients and whisk well. Pour mixture over the fish cubes and coat evenly. Leave to marinate for at least 1 hour.

Preheat oven to 350 degrees F. Roast, bake or grill until the fillets are golden brown and cooked through, basting just once. Serve hot.

Nicole York-Joly
Sherwood Park Branch—05489

SPINACH LOAF

1 French loaf
1/4 C cooked bacon (optional)
1 pkg frozen chopped spinach or fresh spinach
2–8 oz pkgs cream cheese
1 C mayonnaise
1 to 2 C medium Cheddar cheese, shredded
1 to 2 Tsp dill
1/4 C chopped green onion
2 garlic cloves, smashed
Salt and pepper to taste

Preheat oven to 350 degrees F. Cook spinach; drain and squeeze by hand. Mix in all other ingredients. Cut off the top of the French bread and clean out the guts. Spoon in spinach mixture. Place top back on loaf; wrap in foil. Bake for 1 1/2 to 2 hours.

Clair Cinq-Mars
Edmonton Main Branch—03749

SHRIMP 'N' DILL QUICHE TARTS

18 frozen tarts shells
3/4 C grated Swiss, Gouda or Edam cheese
1/2 C coarsely chopped cooked shrimp
2 T finely chopped red pepper
1 T finely chopped green onion
2 eggs
2/3 C light cream
1/2 Tsp dill
Salt and pepper to taste

Preheat oven to 375 degrees F. Sprinkle cheese, shrimp, red pepper and onion into pastry shells, dividing evenly.

Beat eggs, cream, dill, salt and pepper together. Pour over filling. Bake 20 to 25 minutes, or until set. Serve warm.

Note: Could use crabmeat instead of shrimp.

Tara Sohanpal
Edmonton Main Branch—03749

SEEKH KEBABS GILAFI

1 kg lamb, minced
3 T ginger paste
1 1/4 C sliced onions
6 green chilies, minced
2 Tsp garam masala (from Superstore or East Indian store)
2 Tsp red chili powder
2 Tsp salt
3 Tsp oil
1/2 C processed cheese
1/2 C onions, finely chopped
1/2 C green peppers, finely chopped
Tomatoes, seeded and finely chopped
Butter for basting
Skewers

Sauté onions. Mix the lamb mince with ginger paste, green chilies, garam masala, red chili powder, salt, oil and processed cheese. Mix together onions, green peppers and tomatoes. Squeeze out excess water, if any, from the mince mixture and mix thoroughly. Keep aside for 2 hours.

Shape the mince mixture along the length of the skewers and coat with the vegetable mixture. Roast in an oven or grill for 10 to 15 minutes, basting with butter at regular intervals. Remove from skewers and serve hot.

Tara Sohanpal
Edmonton Main Branch—03749

CHICKEN TIKKAS

4 boneless chicken breasts, cut into cubes
2 Tsp yogurt
1 Tsp garlic paste
1 1/2 Tsp finely chopped ginger
1 small onion, grated
1 1/2 Tsp red chili powder
1 T coriander powder
Salt to taste
Butter for basting
Skewers

Combine yogurt, garlic paste, ginger, onion, chili powder, coriander and salt together in a bowl and mix well. Add chicken cubes to the marinade and coat evenly. Cover the bowl and refrigerate for at least 6 hours or overnight.

Skewer the chicken cubes. Roast in a preheated oven or grill, turning cubes occasionally, for 8 to 10 minutes or until cooked thoroughly, basting at least once. Remove cubes from skewers and place on a warm serving dish. Garnish with onion rings, tomato slices and coriander leaves. Serve at once.

Rita Belke
Meadowlark Centre Branch—04329

WATER CHESTNUTS AND BACON

2–8 oz cans whole water chestnuts
2 lbs bacon
2/3 C ketchup
1 C brown sugar

Preheat oven to 350 degrees F. Cut bacon in half and wrap around water chestnuts. Place on cookie sheet and cook about 30 minutes. Place in casserole dish and add sauce; cook for another 30 minutes.

Toots
Edmonton Main Branch—03749

FROZEN DAIQUIRI

1 bottle white rum
2 bottles (1-litre size) club soda
1 1/2 can frozen Minute Maid limeade
3 or 4 limes and lemons, sliced

Mix all together and freeze. Serve at your own risk.

Susan Maksymuik
Edmonton Main Branch—03749

HOT SPICED STRAWBERRY PUNCH

4 C strawberry cocktail
2 C cold water
1/3 C sugar
1/2 C fresh lemon juice
4–2-inch whole cinnamon sticks
24 whole cloves
1 small orange
1 C freshly squeezed orange juice
Cinnamon sticks, orange slices or wedges and wooden skewers threaded with halved fresh strawberries

In a large saucepan, combine the strawberry cocktail, cold water, and sugar. Bring to a simmer, stirring until the sugar is dissolved. Add the lemon juice and cinnamon sticks. Stick the cloves into the whole orange and add to the simmering mixture. Simmer for 15 minutes. Add the orange juice and simmer for 5 minutes more. Ladle the hot punch into glass mugs and garnish as suggested.

Donna Klaczek
Sherwood Park Branch—05489

EASY TASTY MARGARITAS

1 can frozen limeade
1 can tequila
1 can beer
Crushed or small ice cubes
Margarita rimmer

Thaw limeade with tequila and beer (be careful not to make foam with the beer). Mix together in a pitcher. Rim glasses with margarita rimmer. Fill up glass with ice and POUR the margarita mix ON TOP. Enjoy!!!!

ICED TROPICAL SPLASH

1 C diced fresh pineapple
1 C diced fresh papaya
1 C diced fresh mango
2 C light coconut milk, chilled
1 T lime juice
1 T sugar
1/2 C crushed ice

In a blender, combine all ingredients; blend until smooth. Pour into glasses. If desired, garnish rims with pineapple wedges.

Deb Owens
Edmonton Main Branch—03749

FESTIVE CITRUS PUNCH

1 C (250 ml) cranberries, fresh or frozen
1/2 C (125 ml) lightly packed mint leaves
1 bottle (1.89 litres) white cranberry cocktail
4 limes
2 T (30 ml) grenadine
2 C (500 ml) Ocean Spray Ruby Tangerine grapefruit and tangerine cocktail
2 C (500 ml) club soda

Divide cranberries and mint leaves into ice cube tray sections. Fill the rest of the tray with white cranberry cocktail and freeze.

Squeeze 2 limes and thinly slice remaining 2. Pour lime juice into a large punch bowl. Stir in grenadine. Add remaining white cranberry cocktail and grapefruit and tangerine cocktail. Stir well.

Just before serving, add frozen cubes and top up punch bowl with club soda. Garnish with limes. Makes 12 cups.

Tipsy version: Spike this punch by stirring in 2 C vodka.

Soups

Sandra Toner
Heritage Branch—04089

HOMEMADE HAMBURGER SOUP

2 or 3 C diced potato
1 C chopped carrot
1 stalk celery, sliced up
1 lb lean ground beef, browned and drained
1 medium onion, chopped
1 can beef broth or beef OXO cube
1 large can diced tomatoes
8 C water or more
1/4 C pot barley (or rice; barley takes longer to cook)
Salt and pepper to taste

Mix all ingredients in large pot; bring to boil. Add potatoes last, as they don't take as long to cook. (Usually takes about 1 1/2 hours or so on medium boil.) Extremely tasty and great for lunches; a very hearty soup on a cold winter night!! And healthy too!

Cheryl Leverette
Mayfield Business Banking Centre—03839

TACO SOUP

1 lb ground beef
1–14 oz can kidney beans
1–14 oz can pork and beans
1–28 oz can tomatoes
1 pkg taco seasoning
1–14 oz can kernel corn
1–14 oz can tomato sauce

Brown ground beef in a large pot. Add the rest of the ingredients, heat through until hot.

Serve with sour cream, grated cheese and tortilla chips.

Barbara Chandler
Sherwood Park Branch—05489

TURKEY SOUP

Turkey carcass with some meat left on it
18 C water
4 T salt

2 chicken bouillon cubes
1 C carrots
1 C celery
1 C onion
1–20 oz can tomatoes
5 T pot barley
1/4 C lentils
2 Tsp rice
3/4 C fine noodles or macaroni alphabets
1/2 C parsley flakes
1/4 C dried mixed vegetable flakes

Put water in a large kettle. Add all the turkey carcass and the salt. Simmer, covered, for 5 hours. Remove bones carefully from the broth, take meat off bones and cut in small pieces. Return meat to turkey broth. Add remaining ingredients and simmer until barley is tender, about 2 hours.

Jan Peters
Cambridge Bay, Nunavut—06527

CHAR CHOWDER

3 to 4 lbs char, cut into pieces
Chopped celery, onions, potatoes,
  red and green pepper, as desired
1 can evaporated milk (unsweetened)
1/2 C lemon juice
1 can baby clams
2 to 3 T butter or margarine
1 C flour
Fresh parsley

Boil char for 25 to 30 minutes in a little water. Drain and cool down.

In another pot, boil chopped vegetables in salted water until softened. Meanwhile, debone char and add to the vegetables and stock. Add canned milk, lemon juice, baby clams and butter or margarine.

Blend 1 C flour with 2 C water and stir into vegetables and fish to thicken soup. Sprinkle with fresh parsley just prior to serving.

Erna Huber
Edmonton Main Branch—03749

POTATO AND LEEK SOUP

3 T butter
3 C sliced leek, white part only
3 T flour
2 quarts hot water or 4 to 6 C water
  plus milk added at the end of cooking
4 C potatoes, sliced
1/2 C cream (or half-and-half)
Fresh parsley, salt and pepper to taste

Melt butter; stir in leek. Cook slowly for 5 minutes. Add flour and cook for 2 minutes without browning. Gradually add water, then potatoes. Cook 40 minutes. (Optional: add chopped-up green part of leek during the last 15 minutes.) Add salt, pepper, cream and parsley.

Sherry Esch
Commercial Markets—02829

TURKEY NOODLE SOUP

2 C chopped onion
1 C chopped celery
1 C chopped carrot
1 T oil
3 T chopped fresh parsley
2 T chopped fresh dill
1 Tsp dried thyme
2 cloves
1 Tsp ground turmeric
Salt and pepper to taste
3 C bite-sized pieces leftover turkey
3 quarts chicken or turkey broth
1 C broad noodles

Sauté onions, celery and chopped carrots in oil until softened. Add parsley, dill, thyme, cloves, turmeric, salt and pepper along with leftover turkey. Cook 5 minutes.

Add broth and simmer 15 minutes. Add noodles and simmer another 15 minutes.

Kathy Watson
Commercial Markets Edmonton Downtown—03779

CARROT AND GINGER SOUP

6 T unsalted butter
1 large yellow onion, chopped
1/4 C finely chopped fresh ginger root
3 garlic cloves, minced
7 C chicken stock
1 C dry white wine
1 1/2 C carrots, cut into 1/2-inch pieces
2 T fresh lemon juice
Pinch of curry powder
Salt and pepper to taste

Melt butter in a large stock pot over medium heat. Add onion, ginger and garlic, and sauté for 15 to 20 minutes. Add stock, wine and carrots. Heat to boiling; reduce heat and simmer uncovered until the carrots are tender, about 45 minutes.

Purée the soup in a blender or food processor fitted with a steel blade. Season with lemon juice, curry powder, salt and pepper.

Julie Tabler
Terwillegar Heights Branch—04219

BORSCH (UKRAINIAN BEET SOUP)

3 to 4 medium beets, washed and grated (use cheese grater or food processor)
1 to 2 medium carrots, grated
1 small to medium onion, chopped
1–8 oz can tomatoes
3 T sugar
1 T salt
3 litres water

4 T flour
1/2 C water

2 T white or red wine vinegar
1 C whipping cream

Sour cream (optional)

Place first six ingredients into the 3 litres of water; bring to a boil. Reduce to medium. Cover and cook for 1 1/2 hours, stirring occasionally.

After cooking, mix the flour and water to form a thick paste and mix into soup. Cook for another 15 minutes. Add vinegar and cook another 15 minutes. Stir in whipping cream; bring to a boil and cook on high approximately 5 minutes.

Serve in deep soup bowls with a dollop of sour cream, if desired.

MUSHROOM BARLEY SOUP

2 onions, chopped
1/3 C olive oil
3 carrots, chopped
1 T paprika
1 1/2 lbs sliced mushrooms
1/2 Tsp dried thyme
1/2 C pearl barley
5 C chicken broth
2 Tsp cornstarch
1/4 C fresh lemon juice
3 T fresh dill, snipped

In a heavy pot, cook onions in oil over moderate low heat, stirring until softened. Add carrots, paprika, fresh mushrooms, thyme, barley and the broth plus 4 cups of water. Bring to a boil. Turn down heat to simmer and cook for 50 minutes, uncovered, until barley is tender.

In a small bowl, dissolve cornstarch in the lemon juice; stir this mixture into soup and simmer another 5 to 10 minutes. Add the dill. Serve immediately, or for better flavour, reheat the next day.

Pam Scherger
Edmonton Main Branch—03749

CORN CHOWDER

4 bacon slices, diced
1 medium onion, sliced or chopped
2 C niblet corn, frozen or fresh,
  or 10 oz (284 g) can creamed corn
1 1/2 C diced raw potato
1 can mushroom soup
3 C milk
1/2 Tsp salt
1/8 Tsp pepper

Put bacon and onion into large pot. Sauté together until onion is clear and limp. Add next six ingredients. Bring to a boil. Cover and simmer until potato is cooked, stirring occasionally. Makes about 6 cups.

Sara Habinski
Meadowlark Centre Branch—04329

CABBAGE SALAD

1 head green cabbage

Dressing:
1/4 C corn oil
1/4 C vinegar
1/4 C soy sauce
3 T sugar

Topping:
1/2 C pine nuts or sesame seeds (or 1/4 C of each)

Shred cabbage thinly. Mix dressing ingredients together and pour on cabbage. Let stand for 2 hours.

Before serving, fry nuts in frying pan, adding very little oil. Sprinkle over salad. Serves 8 to 10.

Janet Mosier
Commercial Markets—02829

CARROT SALAD

2 C grated carrot
2 green onions, sliced
4 T granulated sugar
3 T vinegar
1 T cooking oil
1/2 Tsp salt
1/4 Tsp pepper

Put carrot and onion into bowl. Combine sugar, vinegar, cooking oil, salt and paper in small bowl. Stir to dissolve sugar. Pour over carrot mixture. Serves 4.

Renal Abou Touma
Southgate Shopping Centre Branch—04359

TABOULEH

1 C medium grain bulgur wheat
Water to cover
4 C (packed) fresh parsley
1 C (packed) fresh mint leaves
2 bunches fresh chives or green onions
Juice of 1 lemon (or more to taste)
1/3 C extra virgin olive oil (or more to taste)
Salt and freshly ground black pepper
2 vine-ripened tomatoes, seeded and cut into 1/2-inch cubes

Cover bulgur wheat with cold water by an inch, and soak for 30 minutes. During this time, use a food processor to mince the parsley (you need 2 C chopped) and mint (you need 1/2 C chopped). Cut the chives (you need 1/2 C snipped).

When the bulgur is plumped up, drain and transfer it to a clean cloth or a double layer of cheesecloth. Wring out excess water; the grains should be moist and tender, not watery. Transfer the bulgur wheat to a bowl.

Add the chopped parsley, mint and chives. Stir in the lemon zest, juice and olive oil. Toss well to combine and season to taste with salt and pepper. Add more lemon zest, juice or olive oil to taste. Transfer the grains to a bed of lettuce leaves or use as a bed for halibut; top with tomatoes.

Luci Reitzel
Mortgage Specialist—10452

POTATO SALAD (French Canadian Style)

10 large potatoes, cooked, peeled, chopped
6 hard-boiled eggs, peeled and coarsely chopped
3 to 4 stalks of celery, finely minced or diced
1/2 yellow onion, finely chopped (optional)
Seasonal green onions can be substituted

Dressing:
Equal amounts of sour cream and mayonnaise (2 to 3 heaping T each)
1/4 Tsp salt
1/4 Tsp ground pepper
2 1/2 T white vinegar
1 Tsp mustard
Pinch of sugar or sweetener

Whip dressing ingredients together until of a smooth consistency, adding a little milk or light cream if dressing is too thick; it should be thick enough to coat salad ingredients but not wet them.

Combine salad ingredients with dressing mix in large serving bowl (pre-chilled). Garnish top of salad with a little sprinkling of paprika and parsley flakes.

Peggy Bensler
Terwillegar Branch—04219

TOMATOES GERVAIS

4 large or 8 medium tomatoes
Salt and pepper
2–3 oz pkgs cream cheese
3 to 4 T light cream
2 T chopped chives
1/2 C vinaigrette dressing (or bottled Italian)
Bunch of watercress or parsley (optional garnish)

Note: The correct cheese to use is the French "Petit Suisse," which is available in some specialty stores; however, I like to use one package plain cream cheese and one package flavoured cream cheese, such as garden vegetable or herb.

Peel the tomatoes by placing them in a bowl and covering them with boiling water for 10 to 20 seconds. Drain and cover them with cold water. The skin now removes easily.

Cut a slice from the bottom (not stalk end) of each tomato, reserving the slices. Holding the tomato in the hollow of your palm, scoop out the seeds with the handle of a teaspoon, using the bowl of spoon to detach the core. (If the spoon is worn and slightly sharp, so much the better.) Drain seeded tomatoes and season the insides lightly with salt.

Soften cream cheese with an electric mixer. Add enough cream to make a smooth light mixture. Season with salt and pepper (if using only plain cream cheese) and add half the chives.

With a teaspoon or pastry bag, fill tomatoes with cheese mixture, piling it up well. Replace bottom slices on a slant, and arrange tomatoes on a platter. Spoon over a little of the vinaigrette or Italian dressing, reserving some to be added just before serving. Cover and chill for up to 2 hours.

Just before serving, garnish with watercress or parsley and sprinkle remaining chives and dressing over tomatoes.

Pat and Monique Turcotte
Area Office—04759 and Northgate Branch—04629

LAYERED SALAD

Dressing:
1/2 C each light mayonnaise and sour cream
1 T + 1 Tsp lemon juice
2 garlic cloves, minced
1/4 Tsp each dry mustard, salt, pepper and sugar

Salad:
2 C spinach
About 3 1/2 C cooked chicken, cut in bite-sized pieces
1 red pepper, cut in strips
4 hard-boiled eggs, quartered
1 small head iceberg lettuce, coarsely chopped
2 medium carrots, shredded
1/2 C shredded Cheddar cheese
3 slices bacon, cooked and crumbled

Combine dressing ingredients. Layer salad in order given, up to carrots. Spread dressing over top to edge of bowl to seal. Cover in airtight container and refrigerate at least 2 hours or overnight.
To serve, sprinkle bacon and cheese over top.

Laurel Skarlicki
Southgate Shopping Centre Branch—04359

BAKED POTATO SALAD

2 T butter
2 T flour
1 C milk
1 1/2 Tsp salt
Pepper
1/2 C salad dressing or mayonnaise
Shredded cheese
6 medium potatoes, cooked

Preheat oven to 350 degrees F. Make a smooth white sauce with the first set of ingredients, then blend in mayonnaise. Dice cooked potatoes into a buttered casserole. Pour sauce over potatoes and mix gently. Top with shredded cheese and a sprinkling of paprika. Bake until cheese is melted, about 30 minutes.

Sandra Toner
Heritage Branch—04089

CHEESE POTATO BAKE

500 ml sour cream
2 cans mushroom soup
2 C grated Cheddar cheese
3 to 4 T chopped onion
Salt and pepper to taste
1–2 lb bag frozen hash browns
1/2 C melted butter
Parmesan cheese

Preheat oven to 350 degrees F. Mix all ingredients together EXCEPT hash browns. Mix well; add hash browns. Put in ungreased 8x8-inch and 9x13-inch pans. Sprinkle Parmesan on top. Bake for 1 to 1 1/2 hours. Excellent to freeze and reheat.

Cathy Werbiski
91 Street and 51 Avenue Branch—04529

SEAFOOD SALAD

1 bag of coleslaw
2 small pkgs imitation crab meat, coarsely chopped
3 green onions, chopped
3 stalks celery, chopped
1 red pepper, chopped
1–475 ml bottle calorie-wise creamy cucumber dressing

Toss ingredients in a bowl, adding dressing to taste. Add freshly ground pepper to taste. Fast. Easy. Keeps well in fridge for a few days.

Anne Ezio
Manulife Branch—04739

BROCCOLI SALAD

5 C bite-sized pieces of broccoli
5 C bite-sized pieces of cauliflower
6 slices cooked, crumbled bacon
1 C chopped red onion
1/2 C shredded Cheddar cheese

Sauce :
1 C mayonnaise
2 T white vinegar
1/4 C sugar

Mix the first five ingredients. Pour the sauce over and mix together. Refrigerate before serving. SO GOOD.

Bernice Tym
Small Business Oliver Square—03420

CHINESE COLESLAW

1 head cabbage
2 green onions
2 to 3 T toasted sesame seeds
1 pkg ICHIBAN chicken soup
1 1/2 to 2 C slivered or sliced toasted almonds

Shred cabbage and chop onions; place in container. Toast almonds and sesame seeds (bake on a cookie sheet at 350 degrees F for approximately 15 minutes; turn often because they burn easily).

Crush ICHIBAN noodles in package and save seasoning mix for dressing. Put almonds, sesame seeds and noodles in separate containers.

Dressing:
1 pkg ICHIBAN chicken soup seasoning mix
1 T sugar
1/2 C oil
1 Tsp salt
1/2 Tsp pepper

Mix ingredients in separate container. Just before serving, mix cabbage, noodles, almonds and sesame seeds. Add dressing; keep stirring, as sugar doesn't dissolve. Toss salad well to mix in dressing.

Chris Buckley
Operations and Marketplace Support—03059

CAESAR SALAD DRESSING

1/2 C olive oil
1 Tsp lemon juice
1 egg
Dash of Tabasco sauce
Pinch of pepper
1 Tsp salt
1 Tsp prepared mustard
1 garlic clove (or more to taste)

Place all ingredients in a blender and chop until garlic clove is chopped. Place in container and let sit in fridge for a couple of hours.

Tanya Ewanishin
Westlock Branch—09399

LEMON-ROASTED POTATOES

8 to 10 potatoes
1 C water
1/2 C lemon juice
1/3 C olive oil
3 garlic cloves, minced
2 Tsp salt
2 Tsp oregano
1 Tsp pepper

Preheat oven to 325 degrees F. Peel potatoes and cut lengthwise into thick wedges. Place in a 9x13-inch baking pan.

Whisk together water, lemon juice, oil, garlic, salt, oregano and pepper. Pour over potatoes, turning to coat evenly. Bake for about 2 hours or until potatoes are very tender and most of the liquid has evaporated; occasionally turn gently to keep potatoes moistened. Makes 8 generous servings.

Pat and Monique Turcotte
Area Office—04759 and Northgate Branch—04629

ZUCCHINI BOATS

3 medium zucchini
2 T butter
1 C chopped mushrooms
2 T flour
1/4 Tsp oregano
1 C shredded Monterey Jack cheese
1/4 C grated Parmesan cheese

Cook zucchini until tender. Cut in half. Hollow out to make boats, reserving zucchini. Melt butter, sauté mushrooms and stir in flour and oregano. Remove from heat. Add jack cheese and zucchini (can also add chopped tomato). Fill boats; sprinkle with Parmesan. Broil 3 to 5 minutes until bubbly.

May be assembled and refrigerated up to 4 hours in advance.

Erna Huber
Edmonton Main Branch—03749

MANDARIN ORANGE SALAD

1 head leaf lettuce
2 green onions, chopped
1–10 oz can mandarins
1 avocado, cut into small pieces
1/2 C toasted pine nuts
1/2 C sunflower seeds

Dressing:
1/2 C oil
1 T lemon juice
1/2 Tsp salt
1 garlic clove, crushed
3 T white or
white wine vinegar
1 Tsp sugar
1/2 Tsp dry mustard

Mix dressing at least a few hours before tossing salad. Combine and serve immediately.

Carrie Lentz
Heritage Branch—04089

GERMAN POTATO SALAD (Warm)

1 pkg bacon
8 medium potatoes
2 bunches green onions
1 bunch celery
3 C vinegar
Salt and pepper

Peel and boil potatoes. Cut raw bacon into 1-inch pieces and cook in an electric frying pan. Do not drain grease. Chop green onions and celery and add to frying pan. Add 1 C vinegar and stir until cooked.

Drain and cube potatoes. Add to frying pan with remaining vinegar. Cook on medium-high heat for 20 minutes or until blended, seasoning to taste with salt and pepper.

Can be easily reheated and additional vinegar added if needed. Traditionally served with Christmas dinner.

Wendy Ewanik
Beverley Branch—05229

SYLVIE'S SALAD DRESSING

2 to 4 garlic cloves, chopped or crushed
1/4 Tsp salt
1/4 to 1/2 Tsp pepper
1/3 C oil
3 T vinegar (1/2 C if you like more)
1 T lemon juice
1 hard-boiled egg, grated
2/3 C grated cheese of your choice (my favourite is Tex Mex)

Mix all ingredients well and serve over your favourite salad combination. My favourite is lettuce with thinly sliced green and purple onion. (The cheese and egg can be added to the dressing or the salad; it's your choice.)

Angie Johnson
Mayfield Pointe West Branch—01599

EASY ORIENTAL SALAD

1/2 C slivered almonds, toasted
1/2 medium cabbage, shredded
2 green onions, chopped
6 mushrooms, sliced
1 pkg ICHIBAN noodles, broken into pieces

Dressing:
1/2 C cooking oil
1 pkg seasoning from ICHIBAN noodles
3 T vinegar
1 T sugar
1 to 4 T soy sauce

Toss salad ingredients in serving bowl. Mix dressing ingredients in a separate container and add to salad when ready to serve.

Barbara Draper
Millwoods Town Centre Branch—04349

WALDORF PARADISE SALAD

3 Granny Smith apples, quartered, cored and cut into 1/2-inch pieces
2 T lemon juice
2/3 C dried cranberries
1 C diced smoked turkey (optional)
3/4 C red seedless grapes, stemmed and cut in half
1 C chopped toasted walnuts
1 C thinly sliced celery
3 green onions, thinly sliced
3/4 C mayonnaise
1/4 C plain yogurt
1 Tsp honey
1/2 Tsp salt
Pinch of cayenne pepper
Several large leaves butter lettuce or red leaf lettuce

In a large bowl, toss apples with the lemon juice and set aside. In a small bowl, cover the cranberries with hot water; let sit for 3 to 5 minutes. Drain well and pat dry with paper towels.

Add the cranberries to the apples along with the turkey, grapes, walnuts, celery and green onion. Stir to combine.

To make the dressing, stir the mayonnaise, yogurt, honey, salt and pepper together in a small bowl until smooth. Pour over the turkey-apple mixture and mix gently until the ingredients are evenly coated with dressing. Place each serving of the salad on a lettuce leaf. Makes 6 servings.

Nick Sackey
Edmonton Main Branch—03749

VEGETABLE GRAVY

- Onion
- Mushrooms
- Green onion
- Fresh tomatoes
- Green pepper
- Cooking oil
- Seasoning salt
- Hot pepper sauce
- Barbecue sauce
- Tomato sauce and paste

Cut the onion, mushrooms, green onion, fresh tomato and green peppers into pieces. Warm the oil in the frying pan and add vegetables. Add seasoning salt, hot pepper sauce and tomato sauce and paste. Add water and keep stirring until cooked. The amount of water depends on how thick you want the gravy to be.

Mary Petro
Beverley Branch—05229

CHEESY BACON POTATOES

- 4 to 5 medium red potatoes
- 1 bunch green onions, chopped
- 2 C shredded marble cheese
- 1/2 to 1 lb bacon

Cut potatoes into 1-inch cubes, leaving the skin on. Parboil for approximately 15 minutes.

Fry up bacon until crisp. Remove from pan and cut into bite-sized pieces, leaving the bacon grease in the pan. Drain potatoes and add to bacon grease along with green onion. Fry until potatoes are tender. Add bacon and grated cheese; fry until cheese is melted. Serve immediately and enjoy!!

Fadia Elbawarchi
Northgate Centre Branch—04629

FALAFEL (Smashed and Fried Chick Peas)

1 lb chick peas, soaked for 24 hours
1 medium onion
1 medium potato, peeled
4 garlic cloves
1 Tsp ground coriander
1 Tsp cumin
2 Tsp salt
1/2 Tsp pepper
1/2 Tsp cayenne
1 T flour
Vegetable oil for frying
2 Tsp baking soda

Drain chickpeas. Quarter onion and potato. Run chickpeas, onion, potato and garlic through fine holes of a meat grinder twice. Add all remaining ingredients except baking soda and vegetable oil. Mix well. Run through grinder once more. Mix again. Cover and leave to rest for 2 to 3 hours.

Heat oil for deep-frying. While oil is heating, add baking soda to the chickpea mixture. With dampened hands, form mixture into balls the size of a walnut and then flatten slightly into a patty. Deep fry, making sure patties are cooked through and are golden brown. Remove from oil with a slotted spoon and drain on paper towels.

Molly-Ann Chan
Sales Market Manager Edmonton

FESTIVE LENTIL AND NUT ROAST

- 2/3 C red lentils
- 1 C hazelnuts
- 1 C walnuts
- 1 large carrot
- 2 celery stalks
- 1 large onion, sliced
- 4 oz mushrooms
- 1/4 C butter
- 2 Tsp mild curry powder
- 2 T ketchup
- 2 T Worcestershire sauce
- 1 egg, beaten
- 2 Tsp salt
- 4 T chopped fresh parsley
- 2/3 C water

Soak the lentils for 1 hour in cold water; drain well. Grind the nuts in a food processor until very fine but not too smooth. Set the nuts aside.

Chop the carrot, celery, onion and mushrooms into small chunks, and then process them in a food processor or blender until they are finely chopped. Fry the vegetables gently in the butter for 5 minutes. Stir in the curry powder and cook for 1 minute. Cool.

Mix the lentils with the nuts, vegetables and remaining ingredients. Grease and line the bottom and sides of a long 2-lb loaf pan with waxed paper or a sheet of foil. Press the mixture into the pan. Preheat the oven to 375 degrees F.

Bake for 1 to 1 1/4 hours, until just firm, covering the top with a buttered piece of waxed paper or foil if it starts to burn. Let the mixture stand for about 15 minutes before you turn it out and peel off the paper. It will be fairly soft when cut, as it is a moist loaf.

Daniel Hwang
Mayfield Pointe West Branch—01599

DAN'S INFAMOUS BAKED SALMON

(Prep time 2 minutes. Cook time 30 minutes.)

1 salmon fillet
1 lemon
2 Tsp dill (fresh is better, but dried will do as well)
1 green onion
1 bunch cilantro

Preheat oven to 480 degrees F. Place the salmon in a non-stick pan, skin down. Slice the lemon and lay on top of the salmon. Chop the cilantro, green onion and dill into bite-sized pieces, and sprinkle liberally on the salmon. Cover and cook for 30 minutes.

Barbara Chandler
Sherwood Park Branch—05489

BARBECUED SPARE RIBS

Ribs
3/4 C ketchup
1/4 C chili sauce
1/4 C maple syrup
1 garlic clove, chopped
1 to 2 T soy sauce

Simmer portion-size ribs for 1 1/2 hours, until cooked. Combine remaining ingredients to make sauce. Coat ribs with sauce and cook on barbecue for 10 to 15 minutes, adding sauce as needed.

Christine O'Donovan (from Christine's mom)
Inglewood Square Branch, St. Albert—08399

SPAGHETTI IN THE OVEN

1 lb spaghetti noodles
1 lb Velveeta cheese, shredded
1 large can stewed tomatoes, drained (reserve the juice)
1 medium onion, chopped in small pieces
Butter or margarine
Salt and pepper

Fill a large pot with water and bring it to a boil. Break the noodles in half and drop them into the boiling water. Stir the noodles with a fork to prevent them from sticking to the bottom of the pot. Boil spaghetti about 15 to 20 minutes until al dente.

Preheat the oven to 325 degrees F. Butter a deep ovenproof dish (about 3 inches deep) generously on sides and bottom (margarine works very well).

When spaghetti noodles are done, drain and put approximately one-third of them on the bottom of the dish. Cover with small pieces of butter or margarine; salt and pepper well. Place half the shredded cheese over this layer. Add a second layer of spaghetti noodles; add salt and pepper. Add onion pieces and the drained tomatoes from the can, cut in small pieces (you may use the cubed tomatoes that are available in the same size can instead). Set the juice from the can of tomatoes aside.

Add another layer of spaghetti, and cover with small pieces of butter or margarine. Add salt and pepper. Pour about half of the tomato juice over the noodles. Using a knife, make cuts here and there to let the juice get through the noodles. Cover with the remainder of the shredded cheese. Cook in an uncovered dish in the oven for about 45 minutes. Serve with green salad.

Note: Using Velveeta cheese can be messy as it is a soft cheese. I have used Velveeta cheese slices on occasion, cutting them in very narrow strips to cover the layers of spaghetti.

Connie Allen
Meadowlark Centre Branch—04329

CARIBBEAN SHRIMP

1 T vegetable oil
2 T finely chopped fresh ginger
Juice from 2 limes
2 garlic cloves, crushed
1 T soy sauce
1/2 Tsp sugar
1/2 Tsp hot red pepper flakes
2 lbs large tail-on cooked shrimp, defrosted if frozen
1/2 C chopped fresh coriander

Stir together vegetable oil, ginger, lime juice, garlic, soy sauce, sugar and hot red pepper flakes. Stir in shrimp and coriander. Cover and refrigerate at least 1 hour or up to 4 hours. Stir occasionally.

Serve with toothpicks. Makes approximately 40 shrimp.

Tanya Shewchuk Brown
Bonnie Doon Branch—04409

ROYAL SWEDISH MEATBALLS

Meatballs:
1 lb lean ground beef
1 C bread crumbs
2 eggs
1/4 C flour
1 T salt
1 T pepper

Sauce :
2 T flour
2 T butter
1 Tsp Worcestershire sauce
1–250 ml can consommé
1–250 ml can beef broth
250 ml half-and-half cream
1–250 ml can wild mushroom or mushroom soup
2 cans drained whole mushrooms

To prepare meatballs, mix ground beef, breadcrumbs, eggs, salt and pepper. Heat skillet to medium-high heat. Pour flour into a shallow bowl. Roll ground beef mixture into tiny 1- to 2-inch meatballs. Lightly coat each meatball with flour and place in skillet to brown on each side. You will likely have to cook a few batches. Place partially cooked meatballs in a bowl lined with paper towel to drain. You can store these meatballs for a day in the fridge if you would like to prepare them prior to a dinner party.

To prepare the sauce, melt the butter on medium-high heat in a large pot. Once melted, add flour; stir quickly and often while mix browns and thickens, about 3 minutes. Quickly add the consommé, beef broth and wild mushroom soup. Turn down to medium heat and stir until smooth and thickened. Add cream and Worcestershire sauce as well as wild mushrooms. Bring sauce to a simmer. If you would like to thicken sauce, add another can of mushroom soup. To thin sauce, add 1/4 C of milk at a time.

Add partially cooked meatballs to the sauce. Carefully stir to cover the meatballs. Let the meatballs simmer for at least 1 hour on the stove prior to serving.

Marilyn Boyce
Bonnie Doon Branch—04409

TEXICAN CHILI

8 bacon strips, diced
2 1/2 lbs stew or round steak, cut into 1/2-inch cubes
2–14 1/2 oz cans stewed tomatoes
2–8 oz cans tomato sauce
1–16 oz can kidney beans, rinsed and drained
2 C sliced carrots
1 medium onion, chopped
1 C chopped celery
1/2 C chopped green pepper
1/4 C minced fresh parsley
1 T chili powder
1 Tsp salt
1/2 Tsp ground cumin
1/4 Tsp pepper

In a skillet, cook bacon until crisp. Remove to paper towel and drain. Brown the beef in the bacon drippings over medium heat; drain. Transfer to a 5-quart slow cooker. Add bacon and remaining ingredients. Cover and cook on low for 9 to 10 hours or until meat is tender, stirring occasionally. Yield: 16 to 18 servings.

Dubravka Staka
Manulife Branch—04739

EASY SEAFOOD RISOTTO WITH PROSCIUTTO AND CREAM

1 pkg frozen mixed seafood, thawed, rinsed and drained
2 slices (approximately 100 g) prosciutto or other cured meat
1 medium onion, finely chopped
2 garlic cloves, finely chopped
1 Tsp basil pesto
1 Tsp Italian seasoning
1 T sugar
1 C parboiled rice or any long-grain rice
100 ml white wine (usually the one you will drink with the meal)
1–375 ml can whole or crushed tomatoes
Salt and pepper to season
1 C water
2 T whipping cream or 4 T 10% cream
Fresh parsley, chopped
Extra virgin olive oil

Cut the prosciutto in small pieces and put into a large, non-stick pan with a heavy lid. Fry with a splash of olive oil on medium heat. When crispy, take it out of the pan and let it drain on a paper towel.

In the same pan, sauté onion, pesto and Italian seasoning until the onion is translucent. Add garlic and sugar, and sauté for another minute to begin caramelizing. Add rice. Stir well to combine with the rest of ingredients in the pan. Deglaze with white wine. Add seafood and mix well. After a minute or two, add tomatoes, salt, pepper, water and prosciutto. Cover with lid and cook for about 20 minutes on medium heat without taking the lid off.

After 20 minutes the rice should be almost done. Add cream and parsley; mix well and remove from heat. Let it rest, covered, for about 5 minutes. Serve with freshly grated Parmesan or another favourite cheese (Grana Padano, Pecorino, etc.).

Laverne Snoek
Heritage Branch—04089

LAVERNE'S CHILI

- 1/4 C margarine
- 1 onion, chopped
- 3 stalks celery, chopped
- 1 green pepper, chopped
- 4 garlic cloves, chopped
- 1/2 lb lean ground beef
- Chili powder
- Pepper
- 2 Tsp garlic powder
- 3 T basil
- 3 T oregano
- 1 large can red kidney beans
- 1 large can Hunts stewed tomatoes
- 1 large can Hunts tomato sauce
- 1 small can Hunts tomato sauce
- 1 small can tomato soup

Melt margarine in a large skillet over medium heat. Add onion, celery, peppers and garlic, and cook until onion is transparent. Add hamburger and cook until browned. Mash hamburger with potato masher. Sprinkle enough chili powder to lightly cover the top of the meat mixture and stir. Add remaining ingredients. Simmer for 20 minutes. Add another light sprinkle of chili powder to top of chili. Simmer for an additional 20 minutes. Stir often.

Heather Wilson-Crawford
Manulife Branch—04739

SHEPHERD'S PIE

- 1 pkg lean ground beef
- 1 large onion, chopped
- 2 Tsp Worcestershire sauce
- 1/2 C celery, chopped
- 2 Tsp pepper
- 2 cans vegetable soup
- 6 potatoes, peeled, boiled and mashed

Cook lean ground beef with onions, Worcestershire sauce, celery and pepper until well done. Drain the grease. Grease a casserole dish and place the ground beef on the bottom. Place the uncooked soup on top of the beef and the mashed potatoes on top of the soup. You may garnish with grated cheese. Bake in oven for 60 minutes. Serves 4 people with leftovers.

Leanne Ponich
Financial Planning—09333

LIP-SMACKING HONEY GARLIC RIBS

3 to 4 lbs spareribs
1/2 C honey
1 C ketchup
1/4 C soy sauce
4 garlic cloves, crushed

Boil thawed spareribs in salted water until tender (1 1/2 hours). Drain and place in shallow pan. Combine remaining ingredients together and baste ribs (can be refrigerated or frozen at this point). If frozen, thaw before cooking. Grill on the barbecue or 6 inches below the broiler in the oven at 400 degrees F. Baste generously with leftover sauce. Turn often, as sauce thickens to form a glaze. Serves 4.

Kent Freeborn
Wainwright—09389

ITALIAN PASTA SUPREME

3 C tricolour spiral-shaped pasta, cooked and drained
1 C grated Parmesan cheese
1 C Italian salad dressing
1/2 red pepper, chopped
1/2 red onion, sliced
2 C broccoli florets
1/2 C black olives, sliced

Combine all ingredients in a salad bowl. Toss gently to mix. Chill and serve.

Gail Glen
Meadowlark Centre Branch—04329

HOT BEAN SALAD

1/2 lb bacon
1/2 lb lean ground beef

1 can lima beans
1 can green beans, cut
1 can yellow beans, cut
1 can kidney beans

3 T vinegar
3/4 C brown sugar
1/2 C ketchup
1 onion, chopped
1 T dry mustard

Preheat oven to 350 degrees F. Fry bacon until half cooked, and then add the ground beef. Fry until browned. Transfer bacon and beef mixture to an ovenproof dish.

Drain the lima, green and yellow beans. Pour them and the undrained kidney beans over beef and bacon mixture.

In a separate bowl, add vinegar, brown sugar, ketchup, onion and mustard and mix together. Pour over top of beans. Bake for 40 minutes. Mix only once or twice; if mixed too much the beans get mushy. Serve with fresh buns and salad for a delicious meal.

Anita Flahr
Northgate Branch— 04629

BEEF STROGANOFF

1 lb beef, cubed
1/2 C flour
Salt and pepper to taste
1/2 Tsp garlic powder
1 Tsp dry parsley
3 T vegetable oil
1 medium onion, chopped
1 pouch dry onion soup mix
2 C water
2 to 3 C mushrooms, sliced
1 Tsp Worcestershire sauce
1 can mushroom soup
1 C sour cream
1–340 g pkg broad egg noodles

Preheat oven to 350 degrees F. Heat oil in fry pan. In bowl, combine flour, salt, pepper, garlic and parsley. Then toss in the beef cubes to coat thoroughly. In hot oil, brown the beef. Transfer to large casserole dish, saving the leftover oil. Sauté the onion until tender. Add the dry soup mix, water, mushrooms and Worcestershire sauce. Bring to boil and simmer for 5 minutes. Remove from heat. Add mushroom soup and sour cream, mixing well. Pour over beef and bake, covered, for 45 minutes to 1 hour. Cook the noodles and add to stroganoff. Serve hot. Serves 4 hungry people. ENJOY.

Karolyn Manning
137th Street and St. Albert Trail Branch—04620

DONAIR

2 lbs lean hamburger
1 Tsp cayenne pepper
1 Tsp sugar
1 Tsp pepper
3 Tsp onion powder
1 Tsp garlic powder
1 Tsp paprika
1 Tsp salt
1 Tsp oregano
1 C bread crumbs

Filling:
Cucumber
Tomatoes
Lettuce
Grated cheese

Soft tortilla shells
Oil
Water

Sauce:
1/2 C Eagle Brand condensed milk
1/2 C evaporated milk
2 Tsp vinegar (to thicken)
1/2 Tsp garlic powder

Measure all spices and bread crumbs into a bowl and mix. Add to meat. Mix well with fingers and knead like bread. Press firmly together and shape meat into a log. Bake on a rack in a shallow pan for 2 1/2 hours at 300 degrees F.

For the sauce, whip milk for 1 minute. Place in fridge for 30 minutes until thickened. Add remaining ingredients and whip until thick, about 2 minutes.

In a low, deep bowl add water until about 1 to 2 inches deep. Add about 2 T oil. Quickly dip soft tortilla shell in water, then put in frying pan at medium heat and let tortilla bake on each side until warm. Meat can be warmed in microwave or in frying pan. Add filling, sauce and meat to tortilla. Voila.

Sharon Mitchell
Southgate Shopping Centre Branch—04359

SWISS STEAK

1/2 C ketchup
1 C water
1 T vinegar
1 T butter
Onion, diced
Pinch of sugar
2 medium-sized steaks

Preheat oven to 325 degrees F. Brown steak in frying pan along with butter and onions. Once steak is browned, put into casserole dish. Mix ketchup, water, vinegar and sugar together to form a sauce; pour over steak. Bake for 1 1/2 hours, covered. For thicker sauce, add more ketchup.

Brenda Sutherland
Heritage Branch—04089

SWEET 'N' SOUR RIBS

2 lbs ribs, browned

Sauce:
3/4 C brown sugar
1/2 C ketchup
1/2 C vinegar
3/4 C water
2 T Worcestershire sauce
1/2 Tsp chili powder
1 onion, diced
Salt
Pepper

Mix together sauce ingredients and pour over ribs. Bake in a 250 degree F oven for 3 hours, uncovered.

Naomi Goonewardene
Southgate Shopping Centre Branch—04359

SPICY SEAFOOD LINGUINI

1–374 g pkg dry linguini noodles
2 T butter or margarine
1 C chopped green onion
1/4 to 1/2 C chopped cilantro (optional)
3 garlic cloves, peeled and minced
2 C shrimp, peeled and deveined
1 3/4 C half-and-half cream
3/4 C freshly grated Parmesan cheese
Salt and pepper to taste
1 T cayenne pepper
1 T ground thyme
2 T cornstarch

Bring large pot of lightly salted water to a boil. Add pasta and cook for 8 to 10 minutes or until al dente. Drain.

Melt butter in a large, non-stick skillet over medium heat. Stir in green onions, cilantro and garlic; cook for 2 to 3 minutes. Add shrimp, cayenne pepper and ground thyme, stirring to combine. Cook for 4 to 6 minutes. Pour half-and-half, salt and pepper into the pan and bring to a simmer, stirring constantly. Do not boil. Gradually sprinkle Parmesan cheese over seafood mixture and stir until smooth. If sauce is too thin for your liking, gradually add cornstarch until it is the right consistency for you. Remove from heat.

Toss cooked pasta into the pan, coating thoroughly. Sprinkle with Parmesan cheese and fresh ground pepper. Serve immediately. Yields 6 servings.

Chrissy Brooks
Meadowlark Centre Branch—04329

MACARONI AU GRATIN

1 1/2 C macaroni
1/4 C butter
1/4 C flour
1 Tsp salt
1/4 Tsp pepper
1/4 Tsp dry mustard
2 C milk
1 1/2 C grated Cheddar cheese
1/4 C fine bread crumbs
1 T butter
2 T grated Cheddar cheese
Paprika

Preheat oven to 375 degrees F. Cook macaroni; drain. Melt butter in saucepan over medium heat. Add flour and seasonings, and cook 1 minute while stirring. Add milk while stirring; cook until sauce thickens, stirring constantly. Add cheese and stir until sauce becomes smooth. Add macaroni and place in buttered baking dish. Mix together breadcrumbs and butter. Spread over top and sprinkle with grated cheese and paprika. Bake in a 1 1/2 quart dish for 25 to 30 minutes.

Jan Waluk
Commercial Markets—02829

OVEN PORCUPINES

1 lb ground beef
1/2 C regular rice, uncooked
1/2 C water
1/3 C chopped onion
1 Tsp salt
1/2 Tsp celery salt
1/8 Tsp garlic powder
1/8 Tsp pepper
1–15 oz can tomato sauce or soup
1 C water
2 T Worcestershire sauce

Preheat the oven to 350 degrees F. Mix meat, rice, water, onion, salt, celery salt, garlic powder and pepper. Shape mixture by rounded tablespoonfuls into balls. Place meatballs in an ungreased 8x8x2-inch baking dish. Stir together remaining ingredients; pour over meatballs. Cover with foil, and bake 45 minutes. Uncover; bake 15 minutes longer.

Cheryl Granger
Millwoods Town Centre Branch—04349

PUMPKIN CHILI

4 C water
1–28 oz can stewed
or crushed tomatoes
3–16 oz cans red kidney beans
1–16 oz can solid packed pumpkin
1 C chopped onion
1 C chopped red bell pepper
1 C chopped green chilies
1 T chili powder
1 Tsp minced garlic
1 Tsp ground cumin
1 Tsp salt

Drain and rinse the beans. Put all ingredients into a pot and bring to a boil. Reduce heat and simmer for 35 minutes.

Lucy Fan
Heritage Branch—04089

BARBECUE SHORT RIBS

8 short ribs

Boil short ribs for 40 to 60 minutes. This removes most of the fat and helps to tenderize them. Drain and put short ribs into the following barbecue sauce in a covered casserole dish. Bake for 1 hour at 350 degrees F. Turn short ribs over halfway through.

Barbecue Sauce:
This can be used for any meat, but is especially good with the short ribs.
1–10 oz can tomato soup
1–8 oz can tomato sauce
1/2 C light molasses
1/2 C vinegar
1/2 C packed brown sugar
1/4 C cooking oil
1 T minced, dried onion
1 T seasoning salt
1 T Worcestershire sauce
1 T finely shredded orange peel
1 Tsp paprika
1/2 Tsp pepper
1/4 Tsp garlic powder
1 T sugar
2 T lemon juice
Finely diced celery

In medium pot combine all ingredients. Stir to mix. Bring to a boil. Reduce heat and simmer uncovered for 20 minutes. When barbecuing, baste meat in the last 15 minutes of cooking. Store covered in fridge. Makes 3 1/2 cups.

Jennifer Barrett
Commercial Markets Sales & Support—02829

BAKED PORK BACK RIBS

Pork back ribs
Barbecue sauce

Preheat oven to 300 degrees F. Cut strips of ribs into 3-rib sections. Line a cookie sheet with foil. Place a single layer of the ribs on the foil-lined cookie sheet (if you have to stack, try to "weave" the ribs). Cover ribs tightly with tin foil and put into the oven. Take a 2 1/2–3 hour nap, read a book or watch the game.

Turn oven to broil. Remove the foil cover from the ribs and broil top and bottom until crisp. Brush both sides of the ribs with BBQ sauce and broil for 1 to 2 minutes. Enjoy! Note: these ribs are so tender, the meat will fall off the bone.

Dana Hingley
St Albert Branch—08399

AUNTIE JO'S NOODLE BAKE

1 pkg egg noodles, cooked
4 T butter or margarine
1 small onion, finely chopped
3 eggs, lightly beaten
1 1/2 C sour cream
1 T parsley, chopped
1/2 C grated Cheddar cheese
1 1/2 C finely chopped cooked ham
Salt and pepper

Butter a 2-quart casserole dish and preheat the oven to 350 degrees F. Melt butter in a skillet and sauté the onion over medium heat until soft.

In a small bowl, mix eggs, sour cream and parsley. Add the onion, cheese and ham. Add salt and pepper to taste. Place noodles in the casserole dish. Add the ham mixture and toss gently. Bake for 45 minutes or until the casserole is set.

Donna Baskier
Commercial Markets Edmonton West—03839

BEEF ENCHILADAS

1 C chopped onion
1 lb hamburger
1 Tsp minced garlic
1–7 oz can diced green chili peppers
1/2 pkg taco seasoning
4 C pasta sauce
1 pkg small soft tacos
1/2 C fresh salsa
3/4 C chopped black olives, drained
2 C shredded Cheddar or marble cheese
1/2 C sour cream

Preheat oven to 350 degrees F. In a skillet, brown hamburger, onions, garlic and chili peppers. Mix in salsa, olives and taco seasoning. Simmer to reduce liquid. Remove from heat.

Lightly grease a large casserole dish. Spread a thin layer of pasta sauce in it.

Spoon a little of the meat mixture into a soft taco. Fold the taco shell up and place in casserole dish. Repeat for the remaining shells until the meat mixture is used up. Mix remainder of pasta sauce with sour cream and spread over taco shells. Top with cheese. Bake 30 minutes or until hot and bubbly.

Wendy Ewanik
Beverley Branch—05229

GINGER-GARLIC BARBECUED STEAKS

4–8 oz marinating steaks (flank, sirloin tip, inside round or outside round)
2 T dry mustard
1/2 C finely chopped garlic (about 1 1/2 bulbs)
1/2 C soy sauce
1/4 C fresh oregano, chopped
1/4 C fresh thyme leaves, chopped
2 T thinly slivered fresh ginger (one 1/2-inch piece)
1 T olive oil
1 Tsp lemon-pepper seasoning
1 Tsp grated lemon rind
1/2 Tsp black pepper

Sprinkle steaks on both sides with mustard powder; set aside. In a medium bowl, stir together remaining ingredients until well combined. Lay steaks in a shallow non-metallic dish large enough to hold them in a single layer. Spoon half the garlic mixture on one side of steaks, spreading to cover evenly. Turn steaks over; spoon remaining garlic mixture over other side of steaks. Refrigerate, covered, for at least 4 hours or overnight.

When ready to cook, remove steaks from refrigerator. Preheat the barbecue to medium-high. Remove steaks from dish; put on greased grill. Cook for about 4 minutes on each side for medium-rare. Remove steaks to a warm platter; cover loosely with foil and let stand in a warm place for 10 minutes before serving.

Felicia B
Millwoods Town Centre Branch—04349

GINGER BEEF

1 lb flank steak, sliced thinly against the grain (other cuts of beef may be used)
2 T soy sauce
2 T cornstarch
1 T sugar
2 T rice wine
2 T oil
8 slices ginger root
1/2 C soup stock
1/2 T sugar
1/2 T salt or to taste
Some cornstarch and water for thickening

Mix meat with soy sauce, cornstarch, sugar and wine. Set aside. Heat wok and add the oil. Add ginger slices; fry about 30 seconds on high heat. Add beef; cook about 1 minute or until done. Push meat up the side of the wok. Add soup stock, sugar and salt. Bring to a boil, and then thicken with cornstarch mixture. Makes 4 servings.

Carolyn Cooper
Edmonton Main Branch—03749

MARINATED FLANK STEAK

1 or 2 flank steaks—1 lb each

Marinade:
3/4 C oil
1/4 C soy sauce
1/4 C honey or brown sugar
2 T vinegar
2 large garlic cloves, finely chopped
2 T chopped green onion
2 T grated ginger root, or 11/2 Tsp powdered ginger

Score one side of the steaks by making shallow cuts in a crisscross fashion. Combine remaining ingredients; marinate the meat in sauce for 24 to 48 hours.

Broil or barbecue for 4 minutes on each side. Slice into thin strips, across the grain. One steak makes 4 servings.

Gloria Pocatello
Devon Branch—03419

PIZZA MEAT LOAF

1 egg
1/4 C dry bread crumbs
2/3 C spaghetti sauce
1 lb ground beef
1 1/2 C grated mozzarella or Cheddar cheese
1 minced garlic clove
1 Tsp basil
1/4 Tsp oregano
1/2 Tsp salt
1/4 Tsp pepper

Preheat oven to 425 degrees F. Lightly grease a 9-inch pie plate. Lightly beat egg; add to beef along with bread crumbs and 1/3 C spaghetti sauce, 1/2 C cheese, garlic, basil, oregano, salt and pepper. Evenly pat into pie plate. Bake uncovered for 20 minutes. Drain off any juices. Spread with remaining spaghetti sauce and sprinkle with remaining cheese. Continue baking until cheese is golden, about 10 minutes. Cut into wedges.

Brad Tarry
Meadowlark Centre Branch–04329

SPAGHETTI SAUCE

1 large onion, diced
2 garlic cloves, crushed
1 lb (approximately) lean hamburger
1 green pepper, diced
2 to 3 drops Tabasco sauce
2 cans tomato juice
1 large can tomato paste
2 T sugar
Salt and pepper
Rosemary leaves
Oregano leaves
Mushrooms

Fry onion on medium heat with garlic, until tender. Add green pepper and hamburger. Sauté together until hamburger is cooked. Add remaining ingredients and season to taste with rosemary and oregano leaves. Add sliced mushrooms and let simmer on low heat for a couple of hours.

Serve with your favourite cooked pasta. Top with Parmesan cheese and serve with garlic bread—and, of course, a good glass of red wine. Makes a large batch, enough to freeze for another meal.

Sylvia Hooft
Meadowlark Centre Branch—04329

ITALIAN-STYLE CHICKEN

4 skinless chicken breasts
1 can tomato paste
1 can tomato soup
1 large onion, diced
3 Tsp oregano
2 Tsp Italian herb seasoning
Parsley flakes
Dash of cinnamon
Dash of cloves

Bake chicken for 30 minutes at 350 degrees F. Place in casserole dish. Combine remaining ingredients and cover chicken breasts with mixture. Add enough water to cover chicken. Bake at 300 degrees F for 1 to 1 1/2 hours.

Shamira Bhimji
Edmonton Main Branch—03749

CHICKEN CURRY

2 or 3 boneless, skinless chicken breasts, cubed
1 small onion, finely diced
2 T oil
1 small can crushed tomatoes or 1 can tomato sauce
1 Tsp crushed garlic
1 Tsp crushed hot green peppers
1/4 Tsp salt
Curry powder (made up of tumeric powder and coriander)
1 Tsp lemon juice

Heat oil and fry onions until golden brown. Add tomatoes. Add crushed garlic, hot green peppers (optional), salt, curry powder and lemon juice. Add chicken and cook in the curry on medium heat until done. Serve with steamed rice. Sprinkle a few cilantro leaves on the top to give it a nice flavour.

Wendy Hildebrandt
Edmonton Main Branch—03749

CHICKEN CACCIATORE

1/3 C all-purpose flour
1 Tsp salt
1/4 Tsp pepper
3 lbs chicken pieces
1/4 C margarine
1 C chopped onion
1 small green pepper, chopped
1–10 oz can sliced mushrooms, drained
1–7 1/2 oz can tomato sauce
1–4 oz can tomatoes
1 bay leaf
1/2 Tsp oregano
1/4 Tsp garlic powder
1 Tsp granulated sugar
1/4 Tsp thyme
1/4 Tsp basil
Grated Parmesan cheese

Combine flour, salt and pepper in paper or plastic bag. Put 2 or 3 chicken pieces into the bag at a time. Shake to coat. Brown with margarine in frying pan or Dutch oven. Remove chicken pieces as they are browned.

Add onion and green pepper to pan. Sauté until soft. Add more margarine if needed. Stir in next nine ingredients. Add chicken. Sprinkle with grated Parmesan cheese. Cover. Simmer slowly for about 35 to 40 minutes, until tender. Serve with fettuccine noodles. Serves 4 to 5.

Note: I use skinless chicken breasts cut up in bite-sized pieces instead of chicken pieces. Doubling the recipe works really well. Very good; my family favourite. A flavourful, zesty meal.

Deb Laurenson
Southgate Shopping Centre Branch—04359

CHICKEN MARABELLA

4 chickens, 2 1/2 lbs each, quartered
1 garlic head, peeled and finely puréed
1/4 C dried oregano
Coarse salt and freshly ground pepper
1/2 C red wine vinegar
1/2 C olive oil
1 C pitted prunes
1/2 C Spanish green olives
1/2 C capers with a bit of caper juice
6 bay leaves
1 C brown sugar
1 C white wine
1/4 C Italian parsley or cilantro, finely chopped

In a large bowl, combine chicken, garlic, oregano, pepper, salt, vinegar, olive oil, olives, capers and juice and bay leaves. Cover and let marinate overnight.

Preheat oven to 350 degrees F. Arrange chicken in a single layer in one or two baking pans and spoon marinade over it evenly. Sprinkle chicken with brown sugar, and pour wine around it. Bake for 50 minutes to 1 hour, basting frequently with juices. Chicken will be done when its juices run yellow or clear when pricked with a fork.

With a slotted spoon, transfer chicken, prunes, olives and capers to a large serving platter. Moisten with a few spoons of juices and sprinkle with either parsley or cilantro. Pass remaining juices around the table in a gravy boat. Enjoy.

Jacquie Burkholder
Morinville Branch—07929

MOROCCAN CHICKEN

1 1/2 lbs boneless, skinless chicken breast halves
2 T vegetable oil
1/2 onion, chopped
1 garlic clove, minced
2 C salsa
1/4 C currants
1/2 C water
2 T liquid honey
1 1/2 Tsp cumin
1 Tsp cinnamon
1/2 C almonds, toasted and slivered

Preheat oven to 325 degrees F. Brown chicken in oil and place in baking dish. Lightly sauté onion and garlic; spoon over chicken. Combine salsa, water, currants, honey, cumin and cinnamon; pour over chicken. Cover and bake for 1 hour. Sprinkle with toasted almonds. Serves 4.

Nadia Umer
Edmonton Main Branch—03749

BUTTER CHICKEN

800 g boneless, skinless chicken breasts, cut into cubes
1 Tsp grated ginger
1 Tsp grated garlic
3/4 C tomato paste or crushed tomato
1/2 Tsp chili powder
1 to 2 fresh green chilies, finely chopped (remove seeds if required)
100 g unsalted butter
200 g whipping cream
Salt to taste
Finely chopped fresh coriander or cilantro leaves to garnish

Melt butter in a large pan. Add chicken pieces and cook, covered, at medium heat for 20 to 25 minutes or until cooked. Uncover and evaporate excess moisture. Add ginger and garlic and fry for a minute with chicken. Add tomato paste, chili powder, fresh green chilies and salt to taste. Fry for 2 to 3 minutes at medium-high heat until fat separates. Slowly add cream while constantly stirring. Turn heat to low and simmer, covered, for 7 to 10 minutes. Dish out and garnish with chopped fresh coriander leaves. Serve with naan or boiled white rice.

Note: Use green chilies according to taste. Green chilies can be replaced with black pepper or cayenne, but results may vary.

Anita Pati
Bonnie Doon Branch—04409

CHICKEN CURRY

2 to 3 lbs chicken, cut into 1/4-inch pieces
5 to 6 garlic cloves, crushed
1 onion, chopped
3 to 4 Tsp curry powder
1/4 Tsp chili powder
3 T canola oil
1 C water
2 to 3 potatoes, peeled and cubed
Salt to taste

Sauté onion and garlic in oil until light brown. Add curry powder and chili powder. Fry for 30 seconds. Add chicken and salt. Stir well and cook for about 5 minutes. Add water; cover and cook for another 5 minutes. Add potatoes. Cook, covered, on medium heat until potatoes are done (approximately another 15 minutes). Serve with steamed rice, pita bread or naan.

Barb Simpson
Meadowlark Centre Branch—04329

CHICKEN AND RICE CASSEROLE

2 1/2 to 3 C cooked and diced chicken or turkey
2 C cooked rice

1 small onion, chopped
6 T chopped green pepper
4 T melted better

2 cans mushroom soup
1 C milk
1 1/2 C crushed potato chips
2/3 C blanched almonds

Preheat oven to 350 degrees F. Sauté the onion and green pepper in the butter. Stir all ingredients together except for chips and almonds. Stir in half of the chips and half of the almonds. Spread remaining chips and almonds over top of casserole. Bake uncovered for 45 to 50 minutes.

Jackie Gill
Edmonton Main Branch—03749

CHICKEN FRANCESE

1/2 C all-purpose flour
4 boneless, skinless chicken breasts, pounded to 1/4-inch thickness (can substitute pork, veal or fish)
3 eggs
1/2 C grated Parmesan cheese
1 T dried parsley
1/2 Tsp salt
1/4 Tsp pepper
2 T olive oil
1 T butter
3 T lemon juice (about 1 lemon)

Place flour in a shallow bowl. Roll chicken in flour to coat. Shake off excess flour.

Beat eggs, Parmesan, parsley, salt and pepper in a small bowl with a whisk or a fork until foamy.

Heat olive oil and butter in a large skillet over medium-high heat.

Dip chicken in egg mixture, letting excess drip back into the bowl. Place in skillet. Cook chicken until browned, about 3 minutes per side. Squeeze lemon over chicken in skillet. Cook for about 1 minute longer. Remove from skillet. Serve immediately.

Vicci MacDonald
Commercial Markets Edmonton Tower—08019

AMARETTO CHICKEN

2 T flour
1/2 Tsp salt
1 Tsp freshly ground pepper
1 1/2 Tsp paprika
1 Tsp garlic salt
6 boneless, skinless chicken breast halves
1 T oil
2 T butter
1 T Dijon mustard
1/2 C frozen orange juice concentrate
1/4 C water
2/3 C Amaretto

Preheat oven to 350 degrees F. Combine flour, salt, pepper, paprika and garlic salt. Shake chicken in this mixture. Sauté chicken in oil until brown; remove to casserole. Melt butter; add mustard, orange juice, water and Amaretto. Pour sauce over chicken and bake, covered, for 45 minutes.

Nick Sackey
Edmonton Main Branch—03749

GRILLED CHICKEN

Chicken
Seasoning salt
Onion
Green onion
Hot pepper sauce
Fresh tomatoes
Green pepper
Barbecue sauce
Tomato sauce
Foil

Wash and cut up chicken. Cut the onion, green onion, fresh tomatoes and green peppers into pieces and add to the chicken. Add seasoning salt, hot pepper sauce and tomato sauce. Mix ingredients and let chicken season for a minimum of 30 minutes.

Preheat oven to 400 degrees F. Bake mixture, turning the chicken pieces over every 20 to 30 minutes, until cooked. Add barbecue sauce and reduce temperature to 250 to 300 degrees F. Cover chicken with foil and let simmer for up to 30 minutes. Serve with rice, potatoes, yams or plantain.

KENTUCKY FRIED CHICKEN BATTER

5 lb flour
1 1/2 C Accent
1 T garlic salt
1 T paprika
1 1/2 T cumin
1 C salt
3 T orange spice
1 T thyme
1 T cayenne

Mix and leave in a container. Use when needed.

Kathy King
Commercial Markets Edmonton Downtown —03779

CHEDDAR APPLE MUFFINS

- 3 C flour
- 2/3 C sugar
- 4 Tsp baking powder
- 1 Tsp salt
- 1 Tsp cinnamon
- 2 C grated aged Cheddar cheese
- 2 eggs
- 1 C apple juice
- 1/2 C margarine, melted
- 2 C finely chopped apples

Preheat oven to 375 degrees F. Grease muffin pans. Combine dry ingredients in large bowl; mix in cheese.

Beat eggs in separate bowl. Add apple juice and stir in margarine and apples.

Add this mixture to flour mixture, but do not over-stir—just blend. Bake 25 minutes.

Carrie Andrews
Southgate Shopping Centre Branch—04359

EASY SUNDAY PANCAKES

- 1 C flour
- 1 C milk
- 1 T oil
- 1 T sugar
- 1 Tsp baking soda
- 1 Tsp baking powder
- 1 egg
- 1 pinch of salt

Combine all dry ingredients. Mix in wet ingredients. Let stand 5 minutes.

Fry in pan or on a griddle.

Connie Silva
Commercial Markets—02829

ZUCCHINI PINEAPPLE BREAD

- 3 eggs
- 1 C oil
- 2 C sugar
- 2 Tsp vanilla
- 3 C flour
- 2 Tsp baking soda
- 1 Tsp salt
- 1/2 Tsp baking powder
- 1 1/2 Tsp cinnamon
- 2 C grated zucchini
- 1 1/2 C crushed pineapple, drained
- 1 C raisins

Preheat oven to 350 degrees F. In a large bowl, beat eggs, oil, sugar and vanilla.

In a separate bowl, sift flour, soda, salt, baking powder and cinnamon. Combine with egg mixture; stir in zucchini, pineapple and raisins. Pour into two greased and floured 9x5x3-inch loaf pans. Bake 1 hour.

Rossana Vojacek
Sherwood Park Branch—05489

EASY CINNAMON BUNS

- 10 frozen dough rolls
- 1 C brown sugar
- 1/4 C vanilla instant pudding
- 1 to 2 T cinnamon
- 3/4 C raisins (optional)
- 3/4 C pecans (optional)
- 1/2 C butter

Just before you go to bed, grease a 10-inch Bundt pan and add frozen rolls. Sprinkle with brown sugar, pudding powder, cinnamon, raisins and pecans. Pour melted butter over all. Cover with a clean, damp cloth. Leave out at room temperature. Turn out the lights and say goodnight!

In the morning, preheat oven to 350 degrees F and bake buns for 25 minutes. Let sit for 5 minutes and then turn out onto a serving plate.

Kim Grant
Morinville—07929

PERFECT BRAN MUFFINS

3/4 C oil	2 C bran
2 eggs	2 Tsp baking soda
1 C sugar	2 Tsp baking powder
2 C milk	1 Tsp salt
2 C flour	1 C raisins or dates

In a large bowl, mix the first four ingredients well. Add remaining ingredients and blend together. Place in fridge. Leave for 2 days (don't stir).

Bake in greased or lined muffin tins at 375 degrees F for approximately 15 minutes.

Terry Lynn Kreitz
Manulife Branch—04739

MAYONNAISE BISCUITS

(almost like Red Lobster)

2 C flour
2 Tsp baking powder
1/4 Tsp salt
1/2 Tsp garlic powder
1 C milk
1/2 C mayonnaise
1/2 C shredded Cheddar cheese

Preheat oven to 400 degrees F. Mix flour, baking powder and salt together in bowl. Add milk, mayo and cheese. Mix well. Drop onto greased baking pan. Bake approximately 20 minutes.

Nicole York-Joly
Sherwood Park Branch—05489

BAKED CARAMEL FRENCH TOAST

Topping:
1 C firmly packed brown sugar
6 T margarine or butter
1/3 C whipping cream
1 T light corn syrup

French Toast:
3 eggs
1/2 C milk
1 Tsp vanilla
1/4 Tsp salt
8 diagonally sliced French bread slices, 3/4–inch thick

Grease a 13x9-inch pan. Combine all topping ingredients in a saucepan. Heat until smooth, stirring constantly. Do not boil. Spread in baking dish.

Beat eggs, milk, vanilla and salt in separate bowl. Dip each bread slice in egg mixture. Place bread slices over topping in baking dish. Cover and refrigerate 8 hours.

Bake uncovered at 400 degrees F for 20 to 25 minutes. Invert onto large serving platter. Serve while hot!

Janis McQueen
Commercial Markets—08019

WELSH SCONES

- 2 C flour
- 1 Tsp baking powder
- 4 T sugar
- 1/2 C margarine
- Handful of raisins
- 1 egg, beaten
- 1/2 C + 1 T milk

Preheat oven to 325 degrees F. Combine flour, baking powder and sugar. Cut in margarine until crumbly. Add raisins. Stir in egg and milk. Pat out to about 1/2-inch thick on floured surface. Cut into approximately 2-inch circles.

Bake uncovered in frypan or on griddle until golden brown on both sides (about 9 minutes on each side). Makes 14 to 16 scones.

Great with jam and whipped cream.

Ruth Shewfelt
Sherwood Park Branch—05489

CHEESE BISCUITS

- 2 C flour
- 4 Tsp baking powder
- 1/2 Tsp salt
- 3 T shortening, butter or margarine
- 1 C grated Cheddar cheese
- 1 C milk

Preheat oven to 450 degrees F. Sift flour, baking powder and salt together. Cut in shortening. Stir in grated cheese. With a fork, stir in milk to make a soft dough. Knead on lightly floured board for just a minute. Pat out to about 3/4-inch thickness and cut into 2-inch circles. Place on buttered baking sheet and bake for 12 to 15 minutes. Makes 12.

Lorraine Haus
Sherwood Park Branch—05489

BREAKFAST ENCHILADAS

1 C cut up ham or bacon
1 medium onion, chopped
1/4 C chopped green peppers
1/4 C chopped red peppers
2 Tsp vegetable oil
2 C shredded Cheddar cheese
8-inch tortilla shells
4 eggs
2 C milk
1 T flour

The night before, mix together ham, onions, peppers and vegetable oil. In each tortilla, put 3 T of mixture along with 3 T of cheese, and roll up. Place in greased 9x13-inch baking pan. Combine eggs, milk, and flour and pour over tortillas. Cover and refrigerate overnight.

In the morning, preheat oven to 350 degrees F. Bake for 45 minutes or until set. Serve with your choice of sour cream, salsa, jalapeno peppers, tomatoes and green onions.

Trudy Nolin-Zoerb
Lloydminster—04238

BANNOCK

3 C flour
3 1/2 Tsp baking powder
Pinch of salt
Pinch of sugar
1/4 C oil

Preheat oven to 375 degrees F. Mix your oil and lukewarm water to make 1 cup of liquid. Pour over all the other ingredients in a bowl and knead together. Do not over-knead. Your dough should be light and not dry or sticky. Flatten with hands in a 12-inch pie plate. Poke with a fork to make air holes. Bake until golden brown. Slice and serve warm with butter, or have as desert with your favourite homemade jam or jelly. Enjoy!!!

Lorraine Haus
Sherwood Park Branch—05489

PEACH FRENCH TOAST

1 C packed brown sugar
1/2 C butter or margarine
2 T water
1–29 oz can sliced peaches, drained
12 slices French bread or Texas bread
5 eggs
1 1/2 C milk
1 T vanilla extract
1 T ground cinnamon

In a saucepan, bring brown sugar, butter and water to boil. Reduce heat and simmer for 10 minutes, stirring frequently. Pour into greased 9x13-inch baking dish and top with peaches. Arrange bread over peaches.

In a bowl, whisk together eggs, milk and vanilla. Slowly pour over bread. Cover and refrigerate for 8 hours or overnight.

Preheat oven to 350 degrees F. Remove pan from fridge 30 minutes before baking. Sprinkle with cinnamon. Cover pan and bake for 25 to 30 minutes, then uncovered for 25 to 30 minutes until golden brown. Serve with sugar.

Kathy Watson
Commercial Markets Edmonton Downtown—03779

BLUEBERRY MUFFINS

- 2 C flour
- 1/2 C sugar
- 3 Tsp baking powder
- 1/2 Tsp salt
- 3/4 C milk
- 1/3 C vegetable oil
- 1 egg, beaten
- 1 C blueberries, fresh or frozen

Preheat oven to 350 degrees F. Mix flour, sugar, baking powder and salt in bowl. In another bowl, mix the milk, oil and egg. Add wet to dry all at once and combine. Add blueberries.

Drop into greased muffin pan. Bake for 15 to 20 minutes. Makes 1 dozen.

Sherry Esch
Commercial Markets—02829

CHOCOLATE BANANA MUFFINS

- 1/3 C vegetable oil
- 1 C flour
- 1/2 C sugar
- 1 Tsp baking soda
- 1 egg
- 1/2 Tsp salt
- 1/2 Tsp cinnamon
- 1 C mashed bananas
- 1 pkg semi-sweet chocolate chips

Preheat oven to 350 degrees F. In a mixing bowl, whisk together oil, sugar and egg. Stir in bananas and half the package of chocolate chips.

Combine flour, baking soda, salt and cinnamon. Stir into banana mixture, just to moisten. Spoon into greased muffin cups. Sprinkle remaining chocolate chips evenly on top. Bake for 15 to 20 minutes. Makes 12 muffins.

Esther Dempster
St Albert Branch—08399

BUSY MORNING TIME SAVER

16 slices bread, crusts removed
Slices back bacon or ham, sliced thin
Slices sharp Cheddar cheese
6 eggs
1/2 Tsp salt
1/2 Tsp pepper
1/2 to 1 Tsp dry mustard
1/4 C minced onion
1/4 C chopped green pepper
1 to 2 Tsp Worcestershire sauce
3 C milk
Dash of red pepper sauce or Tabasco
1/4 lb butter
Special K or crushed corn flakes

The night before serving this recipe, cover the bottom of a 9x13-inch buttered glass baking dish entirely with 8 pieces of bread. Cover bread with slices of back bacon. Lay slices of cheese on top of bacon, and then cover with remaining slices of bread to make a kind of sandwich.

In a bowl, beat eggs, salt and pepper. Add dry mustard, onion, green pepper, Worcestershire sauce, milk and Tabasco. Pour over the sandwich. Cover and let stand in fridge overnight.

In the morning, preheat oven to 350 degrees F. Melt butter and pour over top. Cover with cereal. Bake, uncovered, 1 hour. Let sit 10 minutes before serving.

Kathy Watson
Commercial Markets Edmonton—03779

GOOD MORNING MUFFINS

4 C flour
2 1/2 C brown sugar
4 T baking soda
4 T cinnamon
1 T salt
4 C grated carrots or zucchini or combination
1 C raisins
1 C nuts (optional)
1 C coconut
2 to 3 apples, peeled and grated
1 C sunflower seeds
6 eggs
2 C vegetable oil (or combination of oil and applesauce)
4 T vanilla

Preheat oven to 350 degrees F. Mix all the dry ingredients in a large bowl. Mix eggs, oil and vanilla in a separate bowl. Combine wet into dry all at once, stirring just to mix. Pour into greased or lined muffin tins and bake for 20 minutes. Makes 3 to 4 dozen.

Barbara Draper
Millwoods Town Center Branch—04349

BLUEBERRY CREAM MUFFINS

4 eggs
2 C sugar
1 C vegetable oil
1 Tsp vanilla extract
4 C flour
1 Tsp salt
1 Tsp baking soda
2 Tsp baking powder
2 C sour cream
2 C fresh blueberries

Preheat oven to 400 degrees F. In a mixing bowl, beat eggs. Gradually add sugar. While beating, slowly pour in oil; add vanilla.

Combine dry ingredients; add alternately with the sour cream to the egg mixture. Gently fold in blueberries. Spoon into greased muffin tins. Bake for 20 minutes. Makes 2 dozen.

Kathie Keogh
Edmonton Main Branch—03749

GRAM LULU'S SCONES

1 1/3 C flour
2 1/2 Tsp baking powder
1/4 Tsp salt
4 to 5 T chilled margarine
1/4 C brown sugar
1/4 C raisins, washed and dried or 1/3 C frozen blueberries (do not use fresh ones as they get mushy)

1/4 C milk
Few drops of almond extract
1 egg, beaten

Preheat oven to 425 degrees F. Measure out first five ingredients and mix with hands until crumbly. Add raisins or blueberries. Stir milk and egg mixture in with fork. Flour hands and knead a couple of times. Press into layer cake pan. Brush with milk and sprinkle with sugar. Bake for 15 minutes or less.

Judy Fix
Christy's Corner Branch—04620

BANANA BREAD

1/2 C shortening	1/2 Tsp vanilla
1 C white sugar	2 C flour
2 eggs	3/4 Tsp baking soda
1 T cream	1/2 Tsp salt
2 mashed ripe bananas	1/2 C chopped walnuts (optional)

Preheat oven to 325 degrees F. Cream shortening and sugar together. Next add eggs, cream, mashed bananas and vanilla. Beat thoroughly. Then add flour, soda and salt, sifted together. Mix well and add walnuts; mix again. Bake in a greased loaf pan for about 1 hour.

For Carol on her retirement. We heard baking is your real passion.

Donna Baskier
Commercial Markets Edmonton West—03839

SUNSHINE MUFFINS

1 orange, peeled	1 Tsp baking soda
1/2 C orange juice	1 Tsp baking powder
1 egg	1 Tsp salt
1/4 C oil	1/2 C raisins or chocolate chips
1 1/2 C flour	1/2 C nuts (optional)
3/4 C sugar	

Preheat oven to 375 degrees F. Cut orange into 8 pieces. Put in blender with oil, egg and juice. Blend until smooth.

Mix dry ingredients. Add raisins and nuts. Stir into first mixture. Bake for 20 minutes.

Anonymous
Meadowlark Centre Branch—04329

SKOR BAR SQUARES

1 sleeve soda crackers
1 C butter
1 C brown sugar
1 bag milk chocolate chips

Preheat oven to 350 degrees F. Line cookie sheet with foil. Spread whole soda crackers across cookie sheet in a single layer only. Melt butter; add brown sugar and boil for 3 minutes. Pour evenly over soda crackers. Place in oven for 8 minutes—you should see the sauce boiling. Take out of oven. Pour chocolate chips over top and spread evenly with knife. It will be hot enough to melt chocolate chips.

Raeann Lacusta
Fort Saskatchewan Branch—05839

EATMORE BARS

3/4 C honey
1 C peanut butter
1 C semi-sweet chocolate chips
1/2 bag large marshmallows
3 C Rice Krispies
1 C peanuts

Melt honey and peanut butter on medium heat in a large pot on the stove. Once boiling, add chocolate chips and marshmallows; stir and keep stirring. Reduce heat and stir in Rice Krispies and peanuts. Press down firmly into greased pan and refrigerate.

Note: I often double the batch as it gets eaten very quickly.

Donna Baskier
Commercial Markets Edmonton West—03839

ALMOND SLICE DELUXE

- 31 whole graham crackers
- 1 C sliced almonds
- 1 C butter
- 3/4 C brown sugar
- 1 C chocolate chips

Preheat oven to 350 degrees F. Line 10x15-inch cookie sheet with foil. Place crackers close together to cover bottom of cookie sheet. Sprinkle almonds evenly over wafers. Boil butter and sugar for 3 minutes. Pour over almonds as evenly as possible. Bake for 8 minutes.

Remove from oven and sprinkle chocolate chips over surface. Allow to melt for 1 minute. Then draw lines with fork through the chocolate to make a crisscross design. When cool, put into freezer until hard. Break into pieces.

Optional recipe: Use dried cranberries and white chocolate chips.

Sharron Moffatt
Meadowlark Centre Branch—04329

CRACKER CAKE

- 1 small box unsalted crackers
- 1–35 g box vanilla instant pudding
- 1 large container of Cool Whip
- Strawberry, cherry or blueberry pie filling

Spread some cool whip on bottom of 9x13-inch pan. Place a layer of crackers on top (puffy side up). Blend pudding as directed. Spread half on top. Add another layer of crackers then approximately half of the remaining cool whip. Add another layer of crackers, remaining pudding, another layer of crackers and remaining cool whip. Put pie filling on top. Refrigerate overnight.

Michelle Leung
91 Street and 51 Avenue Branch—04529

CARAMEL SKOR CHOCOLATE CAKE

1 box chocolate cake mix, prepared as directed
(or your own recipe)
3 SKOR chocolate bars, regular size
1 C butterscotch or caramel ice cream topping
1 envelope Dream Whip, prepared as directed
(or 2 C Cool Whip)

Freeze the SKOR bars for about 1 hour before starting to make the cake. Prepare chocolate cake as directed. Pour into 9x11-inch pan and bake. Cool completely. Once cooled, pierce the cake all over with a fork many times (a great stress reliever!).

Spoon the butterscotch sauce evenly on the surface of the cake and let it soak in.

Remove the SKOR bars from the freezer; crush into small pieces. A wooden spoon or other hard utensil works nicely (another great stress reliever). Reserve approximately 1/2 cup for the garnish.

Prepare the whipped topping. Fold in SKOR bits and spread over the cake. Sprinkle the reserved SKOR bits over top and refrigerate before serving. ENJOY!

Anne Ezio
Manulife Branch—04739

DRUMSTICK CAKE

Base:
1/2 C graham crumbs
1/4 C sugar (optional)
1/4 C butter, melted
3 T peanut butter

Topping:
4 eggs
1/2 C sugar
1–250 g pkg plain cream cheese
1 large tub Cool Whip
Chocolate sauce
Butterscotch sauce

Preheat oven to 350 degrees F. Mix ingredients for the base together and reserve 1/2 C. Put mixture into a 9x13-inch pan and bake until golden.

Beat eggs together and set aside. Cream together sugar and cheese; add peanut butter. Beat in eggs and fold in Cool Whip, pour in pan. Drizzle 1/2 C each of chocolate and butterscotch sauce on top. Run knife through and top with crumb mixture saved from base. Freeze.

Note: Peanut butter may be omitted if desired.

Erna Huber
Edmonton Main Branch—03749

MARS BARS SQUARES

4 Mars bars, cut up
1/4 to 1/2 C butter or margarine
1 C marshmallows
4 C Rice Krispies

Melt first three ingredients in microwave at half power for about 5 to 8 minutes. Stir in the Rice Krispies. Put in 9x9-inch pan. Cool. Cut into squares.

Anita Flahr
Northgate Branch—04629

GRANOLA BARS

1/2 C brown sugar
2/3 C peanut butter
1/2 C corn syrup
1/2 C margarine
2 Tsp vanilla

Mix together with a dough hook or by hand.

Add:
3 C rolled oats
1/2 C coconut
1/2 C sunflower seeds
1/2 C raisins (I sometimes use 1 C raisins instead)
1/3 C wheat germ
2 T sesame seeds
6 oz chocolate chips

Mix well. Press into a 9x13-inch pan. Pack down. Bake at 350 degrees F for 18 minutes. Freeze and then slice.

Brad Wersch
Edmonton Main Branch—03749

BRAD'S BAVARIAN BLACK FOREST CAKE

1 Duncan Hines Swiss chocolate or dark chocolate cake mix
1 can E.D. Smith cherry pie filling
1 1/2 litre whipping cream
Cherry brandy or kirsch
Bernard Callebaut chocolate shavings
Chocolate-covered coffee beans

Follow baking instructions on Duncan Hines box; use the High Cholesterol recipe (it gives a richer taste; who cares if it increases your cholesterol count).

Whip your whipping cream. Add 2 T of sugar and 2 T of cherry brandy; whip. If you like the whipping cream to be firmer, add Whip It by Dr. Oetker. Add 3 T of cherry brandy to your cherry pie filling and stir (this gives it that extra punch).

After baking the cake, let cool; then cut into three horizontal sections. Place the bottom on your plate. Spread whipping cream on cake layer. Then add your cherry pie filling and sprinkle with chocolate shavings. Repeat for next layer. Place the top on the other two layers. Spread whipping cream over top and sides of cake, and then sprinkle chocolate shavings on the top and on sides. Place chocolate-covered beans on the top. Let chill overnight and serve.

Sheryl Hunter
Mayfield Pointe West Branch—02829

TOP ME TWICE

Base Cake:
1 C white sugar
1 Tsp vanilla
2 eggs, beaten
1 can crushed pineapple
2 C flour
1 Tsp salt
1 Tsp baking soda

First Topping:
1/2 C chocolate chips
1/2 C brown sugar
1/2 C coconut

Sprinkle on top of unbaked cake. Bake at 350 degrees F for 45 to 50 minutes.

Second Topping:
1/2 C melted butter
1/2 C light cream (half-and-half)
1/2 C brown sugar
1/2 Tsp vanilla

Pour on top of baked cake.

Janet Mosier
Commercial Markets—02829

MARS BARS SQUARES

Base:
8 Mars bars
1 C butter
6 C Rice Krispies

Topping:
1 C chocolate chips
1/8 C butter

Cut Mars bars into 1-inch pieces. Place in microwavable bowl. Add butter. Microwave until melted. Stir well. Add in Rice Krispies. Press into an 8x11-inch pan.

In a separate bowl, combine chocolate chips and butter. Microwave until melted and pour over squares. Cool. Cut into 1-inch squares. Enjoy.

Nadine Dookhoo
Edmonton Main Branch—03749

HELLO DOLLIES

1 1/2 C graham cracker crumbs
1/2 C butter
1 C chocolate chips
1 C walnuts or pecans
1 1/4 C coconut
1 can sweetened condensed milk

Preheat oven to 350 degrees F. Melt butter and mix in graham wafers crumbs. Press mixture evenly into a 9x13-inch pan. Sprinkle chocolate chips, walnuts or pecans and then coconut on top. Evenly pour the condensed milk on top. Bake for 25 to 30 minutes or until lightly browned.

Betty Haugen
Bonnie Doon Branch—04409

BETTY'S (OPAL) CHOCOLATE CAKE

2 C white sugar
2 eggs
2/3 C vegetable oil
2 Tsp vanilla

Beat well, about 4 minutes.

In a separate bowl mix the following ingredients:
2 2/3 C flour
2/3 C cocoa
2 Tsp baking powder
2 Tsp baking soda
1 Tsp salt

Preheat oven to 325 degrees F. Sift above ingredients together well and add to other mixture alternately with 2 C boiling water, beating well after each addition.

Place in a well-greased 8x12-inch pan (I use a 9x13-inch pan). Bake for 50 minutes. Enjoy with a lovely chocolate butter icing.

Bernice Tym
Small Business Oliver Square—03420

GERMAN APPLE CAKE

5 apples, peeled and sliced
5 T sugar
2 Tsp cinnamon
3 C flour
2 1/3 C sugar
1/2 Tsp salt
4 eggs, unbeaten
1 C cooking oil
2 Tsp vanilla
1/3 C orange juice
1 1/2 Tsp baking soda
1 1/2 Tsp baking powder

Preheat oven to 350 degrees F. Prepare apples and mix with sugar and cinnamon. Set aside.

Mix flour, sugar, salt, eggs, cooking oil, vanilla and orange juice with a mixer on low speed for 1 minute, then 3 minutes on medium. Add baking powder and soda and mix for 1 more minute.

Grease tube pan and fill with alternating layers of batter and sliced apples (3 layers of batter and 2 layers of apples, beginning and ending with batter). Bake for 1 1/2 hours.

Barb Simpson
Meadowlark Centre Branch—04329

CARROT CAKE

2 C flour
2 Tsp soda
1 1/2 Tsp brown sugar
1 Tsp salt
2 Tsp cinnamon
2 C sugar
4 eggs
1 1/2 C oil
2 C grated carrots
1 1/4 C drained crushed pineapple
1 C chopped nuts

Preheat oven to 350 degrees F. Place sifter over large bowl. Measure dry ingredients and sift into the bowl. Add sugar, oil and eggs. Beat by hand for 1 minute. Add carrots, pineapple, nuts and then beat. This batter is quite moist.

Grease bottom of 9x13-inch pan. Pour in batter and bake on centre shelf of oven for 35 minutes or until cake springs back.

Cheese Frosting:
1–4 oz pkg cream cheese
1/2 C margarine
2 C icing sugar
1 Tsp vanilla

Mix in bowl; beat until smooth. Spread on cake after it is cold.

Rita Belke
Meadowlark Centre Branch—04329

BLACK FOREST CAKE

1 Duncan Hines Moist Deluxe cake mix, chocolate or Swiss chocolate
1/2 C white sugar

3/4 C water
1/4 C cherry brandy

Filling and Topping:
1 pint whipping cream
1/2 C icing sugar
1/4 C cherry brandy
Sour cherries, pitted

Preheat oven to 350 degrees F. Mix cake mix as per box instructions. Divide into three greased round cake pans and bake. Let cool.

In a saucepan, mix white sugar and water. Boil until sugar is dissolved; cool. Add cherry brandy. Spread syrup on each cake evenly until soaked up.

In large bowl, whip cream and add icing sugar; beat until stiff. Add brandy to cream and beat until absorbed. Place one cake on a plate. Spread with whipping cream and place some cherries on cream. Put another cake layer on and put whipping cream and cherries on it. Put top cake layer on and the rest of the whipping cream. Decorate with chocolate curls and maraschino cherries all over the cake. Refrigerate overnight.

Rossana Vojacek
Sherwood Park Branch—05489

TRICIA'S RICE KRISPIES MARS BARS

3 C Rice Krispies
4 Mars bars
1/2 C coconut (optional)
3/4 C butter or margarine
1 bag milk chocolate chips

Mix cereal with coconut and set aside.

Cut bars into pieces and melt with 1/2 cup of the butter. Once chocolate bars are melted, pour on top of cereal and mix together. Spread over a greased 8x11-inch pan. Melt the remaining butter (1/4 cup) with the chocolate chips and pour over cereal. Let it cool and cut into squares.

Nancy Kruse
Manning Crossing—05429

PINEAPPLE SQUARES

1 C butter
2 C flour
3 T sugar
1 1/4 C crushed pineapple
1 small bottle maraschino cherries, cut up, and juice
1/4 C sugar
1 T lemon juice
3 egg whites
1/4 C sugar

Mix together butter, flour and sugar. Put in 9x13-inch pan. Bake for 5 minutes at 375 degrees F.

Cook pineapple, cherries, sugar and lemon juice on stove. Add cornstarch or flour to thicken. Spread filling over bottom crust.

Beat egg whites until stiff. Add sugar and spread over filling. Sprinkle with coconut. Bake until brown.

Robin Rice
Edmonton Main Branch—03749

ROBIN'S FAMOUS BUTTER TARTS

1/2 C raisins
1/4 C butter
1/2 C lightly packed brown sugar
1/2 C corn syrup
1 egg, beaten
1/2 Tsp vanilla
Unbaked tart shells

Preheat oven to 375 degrees F. Pour boiling water over raisins. Let soak until edges begin to turn white. Drain.

Cream butter and add brown sugar. Beat thoroughly. Add corn syrup, eggs and vanilla. Combine only until blended. Fold in drained raisins.

Spoon mixture into the unbaked tart shells, filling each about 2/3 full. Bake for 20 to 25 minutes. Do not allow the filling to boil.
Yield: 12 medium-sized tarts.

Sylvia Hooft
Meadowlark Centre Branch—04329

POPPY SEED CAKE

Cake:
3/4 C poppy seeds
3/4 C milk
1/4 C butter
1 C sugar
2 C cake flour
2 heaping Tsp baking powder
1/4 Tsp salt
4 egg whites, beaten
1 Tsp vanilla

Filling:
1 1/2 C milk
4 egg yolks
1/2 C sugar
2 T cornstarch
1/4 Tsp salt
1/2 Tsp vanilla

Icing:
1 pkg chocolate instant pudding
1 pkg Dream Whip
1 1/2 C milk

Soak poppy seeds with milk for 6 hours or overnight.

Cream butter and sugar. Add poppy seed mixture. Sift cake flour, baking powder and salt. Add gradually to creamed mixture. Fold in beaten egg whites with vanilla. Pour into layer pans. Bake at 350 degrees F for 25–30 minutes.

When cool, cut cakes horizontally in half. Alternate layers of cake and filling. Cover with icing.

For filling, scald milk. Beat egg yolks with sugar, cornstarch, salt and vanilla. Add slowly to milk and cook until thick.

Icing:
1 pkg chocolate instant pudding
1 pkg Dream Whip
1 1/2 C milk

For icing, beat pudding, Dream Whip and milk.

Chrissy Brooks
Meadowlark Centre Branch—04329

CHOCOLATE ZUCCHINI CAKE

1/2 C sugar
1/2 C butter
3 eggs, beaten
3 C grated raw zucchini
2 1/2 C flour
4 T cocoa
1/4 T allspice
1 C brown sugar
1/2 C oil
1 Tsp vanilla
1/2 C buttermilk
2 Tsp baking soda
1 Tsp cinnamon
1/2 C chocolate chips

Preheat oven to 325 degrees F. Cream together sugar, butter and oil. Beat in eggs, vanilla and buttermilk. Mix dry ingredients and then add to batter. Beat until smooth. Mix in grated zucchini. Pour into greased and floured 9x13-inch pan. Sprinkle chocolate chips on top. Bake for 45 minutes.

Gina Hancheryk
Lloydminster—04238

BUTTER TARTS

1 kg brown sugar
1 lb butter
10 eggs
250 ml whipping cream

Mix ingredients 2 days before.
Preheat oven to 350 degrees F. Place raisins in bottom of tart shells. Fill shells 3/4 full. Bake 20 minutes or until set. Don't over-bake.

Desmond Chow
Bonnie Doon Branch—04409

ALICE'S SPECIAL SPONGE CAKE

1 C flour
3/4 C sugar
1 Tsp baking powder
1 Tsp salt

1/2 C oil
1/2 C water
8 egg yolks
1 Tsp vanilla

1/2 Tsp cream of tartar
8 egg whites

Preheat oven to 320 degrees F. Mix first four ingredients in a small mixing bowl. Make a well and add, in order, oil, water, egg yolks and vanilla. Beat well with mixer. In a separate bowl (large), add cream of tartar to egg whites. Beat egg whites until stiff peaks form.

Fold first mixture into egg whites till blended. Do not stir; gently fold by bringing rubber spatula down, under, across and up through mixture. Turn batter into ungreased 8- or 9-inch tube pan. Bake for about 1 hour. Tilt pan to cool. Enjoy.

Dan Hobbs
137th Street and St. Albert Trail Branch—04620

BLACK BOTTOM CUPS

- 2–3 oz pkgs cream cheese (soft)
- 1/3 C sugar
- 1 egg
- 1 C chocolate chips
- 1 1/2 C flour
- 1 C sugar
- 1/4 C unsweetened cocoa
- 1 Tsp baking soda
- 1 Tsp salt
- 1 C water
- 1/3 C oil
- 1 T vinegar
- 1 Tsp vanilla
- 1/2 C chopped almonds
- 2 T sugar
- 18 muffin cups

Preheat oven to 350 degrees F. Combine cream cheese, 1/3 C sugar and egg. Mix. Stir in chocolate chips. Set aside.

In a different bowl, combine flour, 1 C sugar, cocoa, baking soda and salt; mix well. Add water, oil, vinegar and vanilla; beat 2 minutes at medium speed. Fill muffin cups. Top each muffin with 1 T cream cheese mixture and sprinkle with almonds. Bake.

Vicci MacDonald
Commercial Markets Edmonton Tower Transit—08019

BLUEBERRY LIME TARTS

- 24 baked tart shells
- 1–250 g pkg cream cheese, softened
- 1 can sweetened condensed milk
- 1/3 C fresh lime juice
- Lime zest
- 1 pint blueberries

Combine cream cheese, milk, lime juice and zest. Cover bottom of tart shells with mixture. Add a few blueberries. Top with more mixture and decorate with a few more berries.

Erna Huber
Edmonton Main Branch—03749

CHOCOLATE CAKE

1/2 C margarine
1/2 C oil
1 C water

2 C sugar
2 C flour
1/4 C cocoa

2 eggs, beaten
1 1/2 Tsp baking soda dissolved in 1/2 C buttermilk and 1 Tsp vanilla

Preheat oven to 350 degrees F. Put dry ingredients in a bowl. Bring first three ingredients to a boil and pour over dry ingredients. Stir with wooden spoon; do not beat. Add the 2 beaten eggs and the buttermilk mixture. Stir with wooden spoon until well combined. Put in large pan (a smaller cookie sheet works well—it should be fairly thin) and bake 25 to 30 minutes.

Icing:
1/2 C margarine
1/3 C buttermilk

2 3/4 C icing sugar
1/4 C cocoa
1 C finely chopped walnuts
1 Tsp vanilla

Heat margarine and buttermilk and pour over other ingredients. Stir. Frost immediately while cake is still warm.

Note: I only make half the icing as it makes quite a lot.

Erna Huber
Edmonton Main Branch—03749

RUM CAKE

Cake:
1 C chopped pecans (not too small)
1–18 1/2 oz pkg yellow cake mix
1–3 1/2 oz pkg vanilla instant pudding
4 eggs
1/2 C oil
1/2 C cold water
1/2 C dark rum

Glaze:
1/4 lb butter
1 C granulated sugar
1/4 C water
1/2 C dark rum

Preheat oven to 325 degrees F. Grease and flour 12-cup Bundt pan. Sprinkle nuts into bottom of pan. Mix all cake ingredients together and blend for about 2 minutes. Bake for 60 minutes. Cool. Remove from pan and prick top.

Put all glaze ingredients except rum in saucepan and melt. Boil for approximately 5 minutes. Remove from heat and stir in rum. Drizzle glaze over top and sides of cake. Repeat until all used up.

Note: I find this is a lot of glaze, so I only make half.

Erna Huber
Edmonton Main Branch—03749

CHRISTMAS RUM CAKE

- 1 or 2 bottles rum
- 1 C butter
- 1 Tsp sugar
- 2 eggs, large
- 1 C dried fruit
- 2 Tsp baking powder
- 1/2 Tsp lemon juice
- 1 C chopped nuts
- 1 C brown sugar

Before starting, sample rum. Smooth, isn't it? Now proceed.

Select large mixing bowl, measuring cups, etc. Check rum again. It MUST be just right. To be sure rum is of top quality, pour one level cup of rum into a glass and sample. Repeat again, if necessary.

With electric mixer, beat one cup of butter in a large and fluffy bowl. Add 1 theaspoon of thugar and beat again.

Meanwhile, make sure rum is schtill all right. Try another glass. Open second bottle if nesheshary.

Add eggs, 2 cups gried druit and heat until high. If drit gets stuck in beaters, pry loose with a shoedriver. Sample rum again, checking for tonscisticity.

Next, shift 2 cups of pepper or salt. It doesn't matter which. Sift 1/2 pint lemon juice. Fold in chopped butter and strained nuts. Add 1 bablespoon of brown thugar or whichever colour you can find.

Grease oven. Turn cake pan to 350. Pour mess in boven and ake.

Check rum again and go to bed!!!!!

Peggy Bensler
Terwilleger Branch—04219

BANANA LOAF

2 C flour
1 Tsp baking soda
1 Tsp salt
1/2 C margarine
1 C sugar
2 eggs
1 C mashed banana
1 T vinegar plus
1/2 C milk

Preheat oven to 350 degrees F. Sift flour, soda and salt. Cream margarine. Blend in sugar. Add eggs and beat until fluffy. Add vinegar to milk. Add flour mixture, banana and milk, alternately, beating well after each addition. Turn into greased loaf pan. Bake for 60 to 70 minutes. This recipe doubles nicely.

Hint: Freeze your overripe bananas until you have enough to bake this recipe.

Barbara Draper
Millwoods Town Centre Branch—04349

RHUBARB DREAM BARS

Crust:
2 C flour
3/4 C icing sugar
1 C butter

Filling:
4 eggs, beaten
2 C sugar
1/2 C flour
1/2 Tsp salt
4 C rhubarb, cut small

Preheat oven to 350 degrees F. In a mixing bowl, mix crust ingredients. Evenly spread crust into a 9x16-inch pan. Bake for 12 minutes. Let crust cool 10 minutes.

Mix filling ingredients and spread onto baked crust. Bake for 45 minutes at 350 degrees F. Cool and serve.

Angie Johnson
Mayfield Pointe West Branch—01599

TURTLE CAKE

1 box German chocolate cake mix
1/4 C butter
1 bag of caramel candy, unwrapped
1 can Eagle Brand milk
1–6 1/2 oz bag chocolate chips
Chopped pecans

Preheat oven to 350 degrees F. Prepare cake mix according to directions on the box. Pour half of the batter into a greased 9x13-inch pan and bake 15 minutes.

In a saucepan, melt butter. Add Eagle Brand milk and caramels. Stir until smooth. Spread half of the caramel glaze on the first layer of cake.

Sprinkle with half of the chocolate chips and nuts. Pour remaining cake batter over this and bake for an additional 25 minutes. Top with remaining glaze, chocolate chips and nuts.

Nahid Shaikh
Millwoods Town Centre Branch—04349

RICE KRISPIE SQUARES

5 C Rice Krispies
2 to 3 Tsp margarine
1 jar Marshmallow Creme (it does not have gelatin)

Melt margarine in a large pot on low heat. Add marshmallow into the pot, stirring until mixed. Add the cereal, stirring until mixed. Pour into trays and let cool. Cut into squares and enjoy!

Barbara Draper
Millwoods Town Centre Branch—04349

BARBIE'S MOIST AND CREAMY COCONUT CAKE

1 pkg yellow cake mix
1 pkg instant vanilla pudding
1 C water
1/3 C oil
4 large eggs, beaten

Glaze:
1 1/4 C milk
1/3 C sugar
1 C sweetened flaked coconut
1 tub whipped topping

Preheat oven to 350 degrees F. In a large mixing bowl, combine cake mix, pudding, water, oil and eggs. Blend with mixer at low speed for 30 seconds. Scrape down sides of bowl. Beat for 2 minutes on medium speed. Place in cake pan and bake for 40 to 45 minutes.

Combine milk, sugar, and 1/2 C coconut in saucepan, cooking on medium heat. Bring to a boil. Reduce heat and simmer 1 minute. Spoon glaze over warm cake.

Fold 1/2 C coconut into the whipped topping and spread over cake. Sprinkle cake with remaining cup of coconut. Loosely cover with wax paper and chill in fridge for 6 hours or overnight.

Deb Neilson. Recipe from Olga Laskiwski
Commercial Markets Edmonton South—03399

FAYE'S APPLE COFFEE CAKE

4 to 5 chopped apples
5 T white sugar
2 T cinnamon

Mix well, coating apples. Set aside.

4 eggs
1 C oil
2 C sugar
2 1/2 Tsp vanilla
3 C flour
3 Tsp baking powder
1/2 Tsp salt
1/4 C orange juice

Preheat oven to 350 degrees F. Beat eggs, sugar, oil and vanilla. Add dry ingredients and mix until smooth. Add orange juice.

Grease a large Bundt pan and pour in 1/3 of the mixture. Add half of the apple mixture. Cover with 1/3 of batter, and then add the rest of the apples. Cover with the remaining batter. Bake at for 1 1/2 hours. Check after 1 hour.

Sharron Moffatt
Meadowlark Centre Branch—04329

COCONUT CRISP COOKIES

1 C butter
1 1/2 C sugar
2 eggs
1 Tsp vanilla
1 C coconut
2 C flour
2 Tsp baking powder

Preheat oven to 350 degrees F. Mix together ingredients and drop from spoon onto cookie sheet. Bake 10 minutes.

Laverne Snoek
Heritage Branch—04089

MONSTER COOKIES

1 lb margarine
12 eggs
2 lbs brown sugar
4 C white sugar
1 T vanilla
1 T Corn syrup
8 Tsp baking powder
3 lbs crunchy peanut butter
18 C oatmeal
1 lb chocolate chips
1 lb M&Ms

Pre-heat oven to 350 degrees F. In an extra-large bowl, beat margarine until creamy; add eggs 2 at a time. Beat after each addition. Add sugars and mix with wooden spoon. Add the rest of the ingredients using your hands to mix. Form cookies into balls and place on cookie sheet. Use fork to press top of cookie. Bake on second rack from top for 10 to 12 minutes. Freezes well.

Barb Chandler
Sherwood Park Branch—05489

CEREAL COOKIES

1 C white sugar
1/2 C brown sugar
1 C margarine
1 egg
2 C quick rolled oats
1 1/2 C flour
1 1/2 C corn flakes
1 Tsp baking powder
1 Tsp baking soda

Preheat oven to 375 degrees F. Mix together ingredients and roll into balls. Put on greased cookie sheets. Bake for 9 to 11 minutes.

Candace Wickins
Old Strathcona Branch—04509

OATMEAL COOKIES FOUR WAYS

1 C butter
1 C packed brown sugar
1 egg
2 Tsp vanilla
1 1/2 C all purpose flour
1/2 Tsp salt
1/2 Tsp cinnamon
1 1/2 C rolled oats
1 C chocolate chips or raisins

Preheat oven to 350 degrees F. In large bowl, cream together butter and brown sugar. Beat in eggs and vanilla. In separate bowl, combine flour, salt, soda and cinnamon, and then blend into creamed mixture. Stir in oats. If desired, add raisins or chocolate chips. Using about 1 T dough for each cookie; drop onto greased baking sheet, leaving about 2 inches between cookies. With bottom of glass dipped in flour, flatten each cookie to thickness of about 1/4 inch or more. Bake for 8 to 9 minutes (do not over-cook). Cool before removing. Makes approximately 40 cookies.

Barbara Chandler
Sherwood Park Branch—05489

ROBYN'S GINGERSNAP COOKIES

1 1/2 C shortening or margarine
2 C sugar
2 eggs
1/3 C cooking molasses
4 C flour
3 Tsp baking soda
2 T cinnamon
1 Tsp salt

Preheat oven to 350 degrees F. Cream shortening. Add sugar. Beat in eggs. Add sifted dry ingredients. Mix well. Form into balls; roll in sugar.

Bake on ungreased cookie sheet for 10 to 12 minutes. Do not overbake.

Barbara Chandler
Sherwood Park Branch—05489

SNICKERDOODLES

1 C butter or margarine
1 1/2 C granulated sugar
2 eggs
2 1/2 C all-purpose flour
2 Tsp cream of tartar
1 Tsp baking soda
1/4 Tsp salt
2 T granulated sugar
2 Tsp cinnamon

Preheat oven to 400 degrees F. Cream butter and 1½ C sugar well. Beat in eggs, one at a time. Mix in flour, cream of tartar, baking soda and salt. Shape into 1-inch balls.

Stir remaining sugar and cinnamon together in small dish. Roll balls in mixture to coat. Place on ungreased cookie sheet. Bake for 7 to 8 minutes. Makes about 4 dozen.

Harry Bensler
Edmonton Capital Region, NWT, Yukon and Nunavut—03059

B-52 BALLS

2 C finely crushed vanilla wafers
1 C icing sugar
1/4 C almond paste, room temperature
2 1/2 T Kahlua
2 1/2 T Grand Marnier or Triple Sec
2 1/2 T Bailey's Irish Cream
2 1/2 T white corn syrup
12 oz semi-sweet chocolate or chocolate chips
2 C crushed toasted almonds

In a bowl, mix the wafers, sugar, almond paste, liqueurs and corn syrup; make sure the almond paste is well blended with the other ingredients. Press mixture into shallow pie plate; refrigerate until firm enough to roll into balls, about 20 minutes.

Melt chocolate in double boiler over gently simmering water. Roll mixture into small balls; dip into chocolate, coating evenly. Roll gently in crushed almonds. Place on large trays to harden. Store in airtight containers. Better if aged 1 week (because things seem to get better with age!).

Donna Baskier
Commercial Markets Edmonton West—03839

THE BEST COOKIES

1 pkg chocolate cake mix
2 eggs
1/3 C oil
Preheat oven to 325 degrees F. Mix together and drop by teaspoons onto ungreased cookie sheet. Bake for 8 to 12 minutes.

Kim Bensler
Heritage Branch—04089

LOLLIPOPS

2 C white sugar
1 C white corn syrup
1/2 Tsp food colouring
1 1/2 Tsp flavoured extract, such as lemon or strawberry

In a medium saucepan, combine sugar, corn syrup, and 1/2 cup water. Cook over medium heat, without stirring, until candy thermometer registers 300 degrees F or until a small amount forms hard brittle threads when dropped in cold water. Remove from heat and cool slightly. Add colouring and flavoured extract. Mix well.

Place small skewers 4 inches apart on oiled cookie sheets. Drop syrup from spoon to form 2–3-inch circles. If syrup hardens, return temporarily to stove. When lollipops harden, place on wax paper. Make sure Peggy is around to help clean up the horrible mess that you have just made. Store lollipops in cool, dry place.

Elizabeth Jonasson
Yellowknife, NWT—09879

PEANUT BUTTER BANANA COOKIES

1/2 C butter or margarine
1/2 C peanut butter
1 C sugar
1 egg
1/2 C mashed banana
1 Tsp vanilla
1 1/2 C flour
1 Tsp salt
1/2 Tsp baking powder
1 1/2 C rolled oats

Cream butter, peanut butter and sugar; beat until fluffy. Beat in egg, banana and vanilla. Sift flour, salt and baking powder; add to creamed mixture a third at a time, mixing well. Fold in rolled oats. Chill batter 30 minutes. Preheat oven to 375 degrees F.

Shape batter into balls. Place on cookie sheet and flatten with a fork. Bake 10 to 12 minutes. Makes 3 to 4 dozen.

Allison Gietz
Edmonton Main Branch—03749

ALLIE'S WORLD-FAMOUS CHOCOLATE CHIP COOKIES

1 C butter
1/2 C brown sugar
1/2 C white sugar
1 egg
1 Tsp pure vanilla
1 Tsp baking soda
1/2 Tsp cream of tartar
2 1/4 C flour
1 C semi-sweet chocolate chips

Preheat oven to 350 degrees F. Cream together sugar and butter. Add egg and vanilla. Stir in dry ingredients and add chocolate chips. Dough should form a ball. Instead of using the drop method, form small balls of dough in your hand and place on a greased cookie sheet. Bake. Makes 24 cookies.

Variations: For chocolate chocolate chip, use 1/4 C cocoa instead of 1/4 C of flour. Or use mini M&Ms instead of chocolate chips or different types of chocolate chips (white, dark, milk).

Erna Huber
Edmonton Main Branch—03749

OLD-FASHIONED OATMEAL COOKIES

1 C margarine
1 C brown sugar
1 C white sugar
2 eggs
1 Tsp salt
1 Tsp vanilla
1 Tsp baking soda
1 Tsp baking powder
3 C oatmeal
1 1/2 C flour
3/4 C coconut
3/4 C finely chopped pecans or walnuts

Preheat oven to 350 degrees F. Cream margarine, sugar and eggs. Add other ingredients and mix well. Roll into small balls and flatten with fork. Bake for 12 to 15 minutes or until nicely browned.

Chris Buckley
Operations and Marketplace Support—03059

CHEWY CHOCOLATE COOKIES

1 lb butter
2 C brown sugar
2 C white sugar
4 eggs
1 T vanilla
5 C oatmeal (chopped in blender)
4 C flour
2 T baking powder
2 T baking soda
20 oz milk chocolate chips (chopped in blender)
12 oz chocolate chips

Preheat oven to 375 degrees F. Mix dry ingredients as listed above. Mix in remaining ingredients (mixture is very large and hard to mix with spoon; I suggest mixing with hands). Form into golf-ball-size balls and flatten. Bake 6 to 8 minutes. Makes 7 dozen good-sized cookies.

Barbara Daper
Millwoods Town Centre Branch—04349

SOUTHERN TEA COOKIES (Family Favorite)

1 C shortening
1 3/4 C sugar
2 eggs
1/2 C milk
1/2 Tsp vanilla extract
3 C self-rising flour

Preheat oven to 350 degrees F. In a mixing bowl, cream together shortening and sugar. Beat in eggs. Add milk and vanilla; beat well. Stir in flour; mix well. Drop by tablespoon 2 1/2 inches apart onto a greased cookie sheet. Bake 15 to 20 minutes. Makes 3 dozen.

Robin Rice
Edmonton Main Branch—03749

CHOCO-BALLS

1/2 C butter or margarine
2 squares semi-sweet chocolate
1/2 C sugar
1 Tsp vanilla
1 egg, beaten
1 1/2 C desiccated coconut
1 C rolled oats
1/2 C chopped nuts

Melt butter and chocolate in a saucepan over hot water. Blend in remaining ingredients. Form into balls about 1 inch in diameter. Roll the balls in chopped walnuts or coconut. Chill until needed. Makes 2 1/2 dozen balls.

Wendy Ewanik
Beverley Branch—05229

WEAVER 'HEALTHY' COOKIES

1 C butter
1/2 C sugar
1/2 to 3/4 C brown sugar
2 eggs
2 C flour
1 Tsp baking powder
1 Tsp baking soda
1 Tsp vanilla
1 to 1 1/2 C oatmeal
1 C raisins or dried cranberries
1/2 C sunflower seeds
1 kg (4 C) flax
1/4 C sesame seeds
1/4 C walnuts, chopped

Preheat oven to 350 degrees F. Cream together butter and sugar. Add eggs, one at a time, beating until smooth. Add vanilla. Combine flour, baking powder and baking soda; add to mixture. Add oatmeal, raisins, sunflower seeds, flax, sesame seeds and walnuts. Mix well. Form into small balls and press down. Place on pan, spaced apart from each other, and bake for 10 to 12 minutes. These cookies grow a fair amount, so do not make them too large. Enjoy!

Jackie Gill
Edmonton Main Branch—03749

OATMEAL CHOCOLATE CHIP COOKIES

1 1/4 C margarine
3/4 C packed brown sugar
1/2 C sugar
1 egg
1 Tsp vanilla
1 1/2 C unsifted flour
1 Tsp baking soda
1/2 Tsp salt
1 Tsp cinnamon
1/8 Tsp nutmeg
3 C quick oats
2 C semi-sweet chocolate chips
1 C chopped walnuts (optional)

Preheat oven to 375 degrees F. Cream margarine with sugars until light and fluffy, using hand blender. Beat in egg and vanilla. In separate bowl, stir flour with baking soda, salt, and spices; add to creamed mixture, mixing well. Stir in oats. Fold in chocolate chips and walnuts. Drop by rounded tablespoon onto ungreased cookie sheets. Bake 8 to 9 minutes for chewy cookies, 10 to 11 minutes for crisper cookies. Cool 1 minute on cookie sheet; remove to wire cooling racks. Store in tightly covered container. Makes 60 cookies.

Jan Waluk
Commercial Markets—02829

NO BAKE ALLIGATOR COOKIES

1/2 C butter
1/2 C milk
2 C sugar
Pinch of salt
4 T cocoa
3 C rolled oats
1/2 C peanut butter
1Tsp vanilla

Boil first 5 ingredients well for 1 minute.

Remove from heat; add rolled oats, peanut butter and vanilla. Drop by spoonfuls onto cookie sheet that is covered with wax paper. After they have cooled, you may find they are shaped like alligators.

Connie Allen
Meadowlark Centre Branch—04329

MINI CHEESECAKES

3 pkgs light cream cheese
4 eggs
48 vanilla wafers (or chocolate, etc.)
1 C icing sugar
1T lemon or lime Jello
Topping of choice (strawberry or blueberry pie filling or whip cream)
48 small cupcake papers

Preheat oven to 350 degrees F. Mix 1 package of cream cheese and 1 egg until smooth. Add second package of cream cheese and 1 egg; mix until smooth. Add last package of cream cheese and 2 eggs; mix until smooth. Add icing sugar and Jello powder; mix until well blended.

Place cupcake papers in small muffin tins. Place 1 wafer in each cupcake paper. Place 1 T of cream cheese mixture in each cup. Bake for 15 to 20 minutes or until firm. Cool and add topping of your choice.

Wendy Doray
Mayfield Pointe West Branch—01599

DOUBLE CHOCOLATE CHEESECAKE

Crust:
1 C crushed chocolate wafers
3 T melted butter

Filling:
3–250 g pkgs cream cheese
3/4 C sugar
3 eggs
1 Tsp vanilla
3 squares semi-sweet chocolate, melted
2 T orange liqueur
3 squares white chocolate, melted

Glaze:
6 squares semi-sweet chocolate
1/4 C butter
2 T vegetable oil

For the crust, preheat oven to 350 degrees F. Combine crumbs and butter. Press into 9-inch springform pan and bake for 10 minutes.

For the filling, increase oven temperature to 425 degrees F. Blend cream cheese and sugar. Add eggs, one at a time, mixing well after each addition. Add vanilla. Remove half of the batter to another bowl. Stir melted white chocolate and liqueur into this portion. Into remaining batter, blend melted semi-sweet chocolate. Pour dark batter into pan. Spread evenly. Spoon white batter carefully over top. Spread evenly. Bake for 10 minutes. Reduce heat to 250 degrees F and bake 30 to 35 minutes longer. Remove from oven and run knife around sides.

For the glaze, melt chocolate with butter and oil over hot water, stirring until smooth. Pour over cake.

Maria Russo
Manning Crossing Branch—5429

CARAMEL PECAN CHEESECAKE

Crust:
1 C graham cracker crumbs
1/2 C pecans, chopped
1/4 C butter, melted
1 Tsp granulated sugar

Filling:
16 oz cream cheese, softened
1/2 C sugar
1 Tsp vanilla
Pinch of salt
2 large eggs

Whipped Cream Topping:
1 C heavy cream (35%)
1/4 C sugar
1 Tsp vanilla
1 C chopped pecans

Topping:
2 to 3 T Hershey's caramel topping
1 to 2 T melted semi-sweet chocolate

Preheat oven to 350 degrees F. To prepare crust, mix graham cracker crumbs, pecans, sugar and butter. Press mixture firmly into bottom of 9-inch springform pan.

To make filling, mix cream cheese, sugar, vanilla and salt at medium speed with electric mixer. Add eggs and mix until well blended. Pour mixture onto crust. Bake for approximately 40 minutes or until golden brown. Loosen cake from rim of pan. Let cool and remove rim of pan. For a creamier cheesecake, and to prevent the top from developing a skin, cover with a piece of wax paper while cooling. Refrigerate for 4 hours or until firm.

Whip cream until almost stiff; add sugar and vanilla and beat until cream holds peaks. Sprinkle chopped pecans on top of cheesecake; dollop whipped cream on top of cake using tablespoon. Drizzle with caramel topping and melted chocolate. Keep refrigerated until ready to serve. ENJOY.

Angie Johnson
Mayfield Pointe West Branch—01599

FRESH PEACH PIE

Crust:
1 C crushed corn flakes
1/4 C sugar
1/3 C melted butter
Mix and press firmly into a 9-inch pie plate; chill.

Filling:
3/4 C sugar
1 1/2 C chopped peaches
1 T unflavoured gelatin
1/4 C cold water
1/2 C boiling water
1 T lemon juice
1/8 Tsp salt
1/2 C heavy cream, whipped

Soften gelatin in cold water. Add boiling water; cool. Add sugar to peaches and let stand 30 minutes.

Combine gelatin water, peaches, lemon juice and salt. Chill until almost set.

Whip cream and fold into peach mixture. Pour into pie shell and chill.

Carolyn Mageau
Morinville Branch—07929

CHERRY CHEESE PIE

1 envelope Dream Whip Dessert Topping Mix
1–8 oz pkg cream cheese, softened
1/2 C sugar
1 unbaked 9-inch crumb crust
1 can cherry pie filling

Prepare Dream Whip as directed on package. Beat cream cheese with sugar until creamy. Blend in prepared Dream Whip. Mix. Pour into crumb crust. Top with cherry pie filling. Chill 3 hours.

Carolyn Mageau
Morinville Branch—07929

PUMPKIN CAKE ROLL

1 C walnuts (optional)
3 eggs
1 C sugar
2/3 C pumpkin
1 Tsp lemon juice
3/4 C flour
1 1/2 Tsp cinnamon
1 Tsp baking powder
1/2 Tsp ginger
1/2 Tsp salt
1/2 Tsp nutmeg

Preheat oven to 350 degrees F. Place steel blade in work bowl of food processer. Add nuts; process until chopped. Remove nuts from bowl and set aside. Add eggs to work bowl and process for 35 to 40 seconds or until lemon-coloured. With machine running, add granulated sugar; process until mixture combines and is slightly thickened. Add pumpkin and lemon juice; process with on and off turns until mixed. Stir together flour, cinnamon, baking powder, ginger, salt and nutmeg; add to work bowl. Process with 2 or 3 on and off turns, just until flour disappears. Do not over-mix.

Spread batter in a greased and floured 10x15x1-inch baking pan. Sprinkle with the chopped walnuts. Bake for 15 minutes. Turn out onto towel sprinkled with powdered sugar. Start at narrow end; roll up cake and towel together so nuts are on outside of roll. Cool, seam side down, on rack for about 5 to 10 minutes.

Cream Cheese Filling:
125 g cream cheese
1/2 Tsp vanilla
1 Tsp butter
3/8 C powdered sugar

Beat first three ingredients until smooth; then add sugar. Beat until smooth. Unroll cake and spread mixture on cake. Re-roll; chill 2 hours. Can be frozen.

Donna Baskier
Commercial Markets Edmonton West—03839

APPLE CRISP

6 apples, peeled and sliced
2/3 C flour
1 C brown sugar
1/2 C oatmeal
1/2 C margarine

Preheat oven to 350 degrees F. Put sliced apples into ungreased 9x9-inch baking dish. In a large bowl, mix remaining ingredients together with your hands. Spread over apples. Bake for 30 minutes or until golden brown.

Variation: This recipe works well with peaches or canned pie filling.

Fadia Elbawarchi
Northgate Branch—04629

BAKLAWA

2 pkgs fillo dough

Filling:

2 lbs walnuts
3/4 C sugar
2 T orange blossom water (Mazahar—can be purchased at any Middle Eastern or Greek specialty store)
2 1/2 lbs butter

Syrup:
3 C sugar
2 C water
2 T orange blossom water
2 T lemon juice

Unwrap and carefully unfold thawed fillo dough; cover with plastic wrap or wax paper and a damp cloth to keep the dough from drying out.

For the filling, grind the walnuts coarsely; mix with sugar and orange blossom water until well blended. Butter a 12x16-inch baking pan. Render the butter.

To assemble, layer one package of fillo sheets in the pan, buttering generously between each sheet with a pastry brush or cloth dipped in butter. Mix 2 to 3 T water with the walnut mixture and put over the top of the last sheet, making sure to keep the layer of walnuts level.

Repeat the same procedure with the second package of dough, buttering generously between each sheet, and on the top. Cut into diamonds, dipping the knife into hot water as you go for easier cutting. Pour any remaining butter over top.

Bake at 350 degrees F for 45 minutes to 1 hour (depending on your oven) or until bottom is done and top is golden brown. If top does not brown nicely, put the baklawa under the broiler for a few seconds, watching constantly, as it will burn very quickly.

For the syrup, mix sugar and water together and bring to a boil. Boil about 15 to 20 minutes. Remove syrup from heat. Add lemon juice and orange blossom water. Stir and let cool.

Tip: Syrup must either be cool and poured over hot baklawa or hot and poured over cooled baklawa. Never pour hot syrup over hot baklawa; it will make it soggy.

Shortcut: Butter pan and place one whole package of fillo dough in pan, butter top, and add nut filling. Place second package of fillo dough over nuts and butter the top. Cut into diamonds and pour all the rendered butter into the pan, making sure it settles into all the cuts and around edges. Bake as directed above.

Shirley Windross
Edmonton Main Branch —03749

CHOCOLATE LAYER DESSERT

1 C chopped pecans
1 C flour
1/2 C butter or margarine, melted
1–8 oz pkg cream cheese
1 C icing sugar
3 small tubs Cool Whip
1 small pkg instant chocolate pudding
1 small pkg instant vanilla pudding
3 C milk

Layer 1: Combine pecans, flour and melted butter or margarine. Press into a 9x13-inch pan. Bake at 350 degrees F for 25 minutes. Cool.

Layer 2: Whip together cream cheese, icing sugar and 1 small tub of Cool Whip. Spread over cooled base.

Layer 3: Combine the two puddings together with milk until thick. Spread over the cheese layer. Spread with 2 small tubs of Cool Whip. Top with shaved chocolate. Chill well before serving. Freezes well.

Erna Huber
Edmonton Main Branch—03749

LEMON CHEESECAKE

Crust:
1 3/4 C graham wafer crumbs, approximately
1/3 C butter
1 T sugar

Preheat oven to 350 degrees F. Mix together above ingredients. Place in a 9x13-inch pan and bake for 15 to 20 minutes.

1 1/2 pkg cream cheese
1 C sugar
1 Tsp vanilla

1 small pkg lemon Jello
1 C hot water
4 T lemon juice

1 large can evaporated milk (well chilled)
2 T lemon juice

Add Jello to hot water with lemon juice and stir until dissolved. Cool until stiff.

Mix cream cheese with sugar and vanilla. Beat Jello slightly and mix in with cream cheese mixture. Beat evaporated milk for 1 minute, add the 2 T lemon juice, and then continue beating until stiff. Evaporated milk must be VERY cold. Add beaten lemon and cheese mixture to milk; blend. Pour into 9x13-inch pan (over graham wafer crust) and chill for about 4 hours before serving.

Wendy Hildebrandt
Edmonton Main Branch—03749

CHOCOLATE DESSERT

1 envelope Dream Whip
1 large instant chocolate pudding mix
1 1/4 C chocolate wafer crumbs
1/4 C melted margarine

Prepare Dream Whip and chocolate pudding. Fold the Dream Whip into the chocolate pudding. Set aside.

Combine chocolate wafer crumbs and melted margarine. Save 3 T of mixture for the top. Put wafer crumbs into 8x8-inch pan and press firmly to form a crust. Spoon prepared chocolate mixture into pan. Sprinkle with remaining crumbs. Chill and serve.

A very nice and light dessert, a favourite of our family. I double the recipe and it works fine, except there is extra pudding mixture when you're done, but that tastes good on its own. Regular-size recipe serves 8.

Deb Owens
Edmonton Main Branch—03749

PEPPERMINT CHEESECAKE

1 C chocolate wafer crumbs
3 T margarine, melted

1 envelope unflavoured gelatin
1/4 C cold water
2–250 g pkgs cream cheese
1/2 C sugar
1/2 C milk
2/3 C crushed peppermint candy (I use candy canes)
1 C whipping cream, whipped
3 Areo chocolate bars, finely chopped
Red food colouring, optional

Preheat oven to 350 degrees F. Combine crumbs and margarine and press onto bottom of 9-inch springform pan. Bake 10 minutes. Cool.

Soften gelatin in cold water; stir over low heat until dissolved. Combine cream cheese and sugar, mixing with electric mixer until well blended. Gradually add gelatin, milk and peppermint candy, mixing until well blended; chill until slightly thickened.

Fold in whipped cream and chocolate. If desired, fold in a few drops of red food colouring to tint mixture pink. Pour over crust; chill until firm.

Before serving, garnish with additional whipped cream, peppermint candy and chocolate wafer crumbs.

Anne Taylor
Small Business Edmonton

RASPBERRY FREEZE

1 C chocolate wafer crumbs
2 T butter or margarine, melted
1 pkg cream cheese, softened
1 can frozen concentrated raspberry juice, thawed
2 T icing sugar
1 container Cool Whip

Combine crumbs and butter and press onto bottom of a 9-inch springform pan. Place crust in freezer for 15 minutes.

Place cream cheese, raspberry concentrate and icing sugar in blender. Beat on high speed until smooth. Pour into large bowl and fold in whipped topping. Pour over crust. Freeze until firm (about 4 hours). Remove from freezer 10 minutes before serving. Makes 10 to 12 servings.

CROWN JEWEL DESSERT

1–3 oz pkg orange Jello
1–3 oz pkg cherry Jello
1–3 oz pkg lime Jello
3 C boiling water
1–3 oz pkg lemon Jello
1 C boiling water
1/2 C canned pineapple juice
1 1/2 C graham wafers
1/3 C melted butter
2 envelopes Dream Whip

Prepare the orange, cherry, lime Jello powders separately using 1 cup boiling water and 1/2 C cold water for each. Pour into separate 8-inch square pans. Chill until firm—at least 3 hours or overnight. Cut into 1/2-inch cubes.

Dissolve lemon Jello powder in 1 C boiling water; stir in pineapple juice. Chill until slightly thickened.

Meanwhile, mix the crumbs and the melted butter; press into bottom of 9x13-inch pan. Prepare Dream Whip as directed on package. Fold into slightly thickened lemon jelly. Fold in jelly cubes. Spoon into prepared pan and chill until firm, about 5 hours. Makes 12 servings.

Mary Wilson
Edmonton Main Branch—03749

MIXED BERRY CHEESE TORTE

Crust:
1 3/4 C flour
1/2 C sugar
1/2 Tsp baking powder
1/2 Tsp baking soda
1/4 Tsp salt
3/4 C margarine
2 eggs
1 Tsp vanilla

Filling:
1–250 g pkg cream cheese, softened
1 egg
1/4 C sugar
1 can E.D. Smith mixed berry pie filling, divided

Preheat oven to 350 degrees F. Grease a 10-inch springform pan. Dust lightly with flour. Combine all ingredients for crust in a large mixer bowl. Beat at medium speed of electric mixer until smooth, about 2 minutes. Spread batter over bottom and 2 inches up sides of prepared pan.

For the filling, beat cream cheese, egg and sugar together in a small bowl at medium speed until smooth and creamy. Reserve 1/4 C pie filling for top, and then spread remainder in the prepared crust. Pour cheese mixture evenly on top. Spoon remaining pie filling evenly over top of cheese mixture. Bake for 45 to 55 minutes, or until set and light golden brown. Serve slightly warm or cool.

Shahida Saleem
Edmonton Main Branch—03749

ICE CREAM SHOP TOFFEE BAR CRUNCH PIE

1/3 C butterscotch sauce
1–9-inch graham wafer crumb crust
1 1/2 C cold half-and-half cream or milk
1 pkg vanilla Jello instant pudding
3 1/2 C thawed Cool Whip
1 C chopped chocolate-covered toffee butter crunch bars (about 4–39 g bars)

Pour butterscotch sauce onto bottom of crumb crust and spread evenly over crust. Prepare pudding mix with cream as directed on package. Stir whipped topping and chopped toffee bar into pudding, reserving 2 T of toffee bar for garnish. Spoon mixture into crumb crust. Place pie into freezer for 6 hours.

Remove pie 10 minutes before serving. Decorate with remaining toffee bar. Pie may be stored in freezer for up to 1 month.

Ken Carter
Edmonton—03420

HALF HOUR PUDDING

2 T butter
1/2 C brown sugar
1 C flour
1/2 C raisins
1/2 C milk
1 Tsp baking powder

Preheat the oven to 400 degrees F. Mix the above ingredients together and put into a greased casserole pan. Mix the following:

1/2 C brown sugar
3/4 C boiling water
1 Tsp butter
1/4 Tsp nutmeg

Pour over the batter in the casserole pan and cook for 30 minutes.

LIST OF CONTRIBUTORS

Connie Allen
Carrie Andrews
Felicia B
Jennifer Barrett
Donna Baskier
Kim Bensler
Harry Bensler
Peggy Bensler
Shamira Bhimji
Marilyn Boyce
Chrissy Brooks
Myrna Buck
Chris Buckley
Jacquie Burkholder
Ken Carter
Molly-Ann Chan
Barbara Chandler
Desmond Chow
Carolyn Cooper
Wendy Doray
Esther Dempster
Nadine Dookhoo
Barbara Draper
Fadia Elbawarchi
Wendy Ewanik
Tanya Ewanishin
Sherry Esch
Anne Ezio
Lucy Fan
Judy Fix
Anita Flahr
Kent Freeborn
Audrey Fredrickson
Allison Gietz
Jackie Gill
Gail Glen
Naomi Goonewardene
Cheryl Granger
Kim Grant
Sara Habinski
Jo Halaby
Gina Hancheryk
Betty Haugen
Lorraine Haus
Wendy Hildebrandt
Dana Hingley
Dan Hobbs
Sylvia Hooft
Erna Huber
Sheryl Hunter
Daniel Hwang
Jessica
Angie Johnson
Elizabeth Jonasson
Kathie Keogh
Kathy King
Donna Klaczek
Terry Lynn Kreitz
Nancy Kruse
Raeann Lacusta
Jennifer Langley
Deb Laurenson
Allison Laursen
Michelle Leung
Carrie Lentz
Cheryl Leverette
Carolyn Mageau
Susan Maksymuik
Vicci MacDonald
Karolyn Manning
Janis McQueen
Pam Meaver
Sharon Mitchell
Sharron Moffatt
Sharon Mohr
Janet Mosier
Deb Neilson
Trudy Nolin-Zoerb
Christine O'Donovan
Deb Owens
Anita Pati
Jan Peters
Mary Petro
Gloria Pocatello
Leanne Ponich
Luci Reitzel
Robin Rice
Maria Russo
Nick Sackey
Shahida Saleem
Pam Scherger
Nahid Shaikh
Tanya Shewchuk Brown
Ruth Shewfelt
Connie Silva
Barb Simpson
Laurel Skarlicki
Lahni Smith
Laverne Snoek
Alison Soby
Dubravka Staka
Brenda Sutherland
Julie Tabler
Brad Tarry
Anne Taylor
Toots
Sandra Toner
Renal Abou Tourma
Pat and Monique Turcotte
Bernice Tym
Nadia Umer
Rossana Vojacek
Jan Waluk
Kathy Watson
Cathy Werbiski
Brad Wersch
Candace Wickins
Mary Wilson
Heather Wilson-Crawford
Shirley Windross
Nicole York-Joly

INDEX